The Next 52 Weeks
*One Year to Transform
Your Work Environment*

Phillip B. Wilson
LRI Management Services, Inc.
Broken Arrow, Oklahoma

To
Mom, my rock
Dad, my inspiration
Janet and Marissa, my life

Acknowledgements

There are a number of people without whom this book would not be possible.

This book is dedicated to the four people who are the most important in my life and without whom I would not accomplish anything. My wife, Janet, has listened to me talk about this book almost as long as we have known each other. She made great suggestions about how to structure the book – especially the sidebars about client stories. She has encouraged me every step of the way. She also gave me the greatest gift I have ever received – our daughter Marissa. Janet is my best friend and I am the luckiest man in the world to have her as my wife.

My Mom gets the lion's share of credit for anything I accomplish. She made great sacrifices to make sure that my brothers and I grew up unconditionally loved. She inspired (okay, sometimes it was more like "required") us to perform whatever we did to the best of our capabilities. In addition to whatever natural gifts I got from her, she taught me the importance of hard work, perseverance and staying positive. She is simply the greatest mother a boy has ever had.

My Dad is my inspiration, and the star I gaze at when dreaming about what my life can be. He has been a great mentor, both professionally and personally. He has inspired much of my professional work – including the title and much of my early thinking about this book. He is my partner at work and my friend all the time. I am truly blessed to have him for my father.

Whatever clarity of thinking is found in this text I attribute to my experience as a debater in high school and college. Two of the most important influences in my life are my debate coaches, Jeanne DeVilliers and David Snowball. They taught me how to reason, persuade and communicate clearly. If this book fails in any of these regards it is due to the student, not the teachers.

Much of my thinking about employee relations issues I attribute to my mentor, Dick Wessels. I learned a lot from Dick while a lawyer at his firm. Many of these were the traditional lessons learned while bantering about mind-numbing and obscure legal issues around the office. Yet he taught me much more by letting me watch him and giving me the freedom to learn by doing. Dick gave me opportunities that I didn't deserve, that let me make huge strides up a pretty steep learning curve. Although I only worked for Dick about three years, much of what I have learned since is often a variation on a theme that I discovered while with him.

Finally, I could not have completed he actual work of this book without help from my three assistants, Kileen Heidenreiter, Glenda Mims and Judy Barnett. They typed, proofread and commented on drafts of this book. I also thank Nancy Bizjack, my editor, whose comments and corrections were an immense help. The book is much improved due to their help.

Preface

"Whatever you can do or dream you can do, begin it.
Boldness has genius, power and magic in it.
Begin it now."
Johann Wolfgang Goethe

This book, like many others, is about transformation
and change. My focus is on change in organizations;
more specifically about transforming employee
relations environments in companies that have
recently won union organizing campaigns. Yet
fundamentally its lessons are about moving any group
from a state of negative energy to one of positive
energy.

Physics teaches that it takes a considerable amount of
energy to change direction or momentum, much more
than it takes to simply continue going in the same
direction. The same thing is true with organizations.

In organizations this means it is much easier to stay
mired in negativity (complaining, second-guessing
and undermining others) than to change direction and
become positive. In my experience, when it comes to
organizational change, the physics equations may be
too optimistic.

Once an organization has altered its course and
achieved some positive gains, a new momentum is
established. This creates momentum just as powerful
as that which reinforced the negative environment.
The goal of this book is to teach you some principles

for creating this energy shift that is so elusive for some organizations.

We often look for quick fixes and instant gratification. Give us something in a box that will solve all of our problems, but only if it will work by the end of the day. Most of the time the promise of the quick fix is a myth; it is almost always a myth in organizations. Certainly there are some changes that can have an immediate impact on the morale of a company (a leadership change or a new line of business, for example) but these changes do not, by themselves, create enough energy to change the momentum of an organization.

It is fashionable today (some would argue not fashionable enough) to fire the CEO when a company fails to reach its financial goals. The theory is that a new leader can breathe life into the organization and "turn it around." Often the new arrival does create a splash, both on Wall Street and in the company. But these changes are often short-lived. That is because more energy is needed to create lasting change; the momentum of negativity can be very difficult to counter.

Organizations are simply an amalgam of all the human relationships that exist between and among all the members of that community. Each interaction between each person is a brief example of what the larger organization represents, what it is. These interactions **are** the organization.

Big changes can alter the interactions among the members of a community, but that does not in and of itself change the organization. Instead, these interactions must become habit, a permanent alteration of the way members interact with one another. Only then can one say that the community has changed.

You are what you do every day. Organizations are what their community members do every day. Going on a crash diet might help you lose weight, but to maintain that weight loss you must change your daily habits of exercise and eating. Likewise, leadership changes, downsizing and change programs may create a period of improved performance in an organization (oftentimes even this does not occur). However, if the daily habits and interactions of community-members do not change, these organizations, like the individuals that define them, will slip back into bad habits.

This book, then, is not about a corporate change program or initiative to improve employee relations environments. Instead, it is about habits organization members can adopt, particularly habits in dealing with employee problems, that will eventually improve the overall employee relations environment in an organization. This is not a quick fix. It is not something you can do for a while. It is definitely not easy.

The good news is that these new habits, by definition, create new relationships, new possibilities and new organizations. They create their own momentum. Only by changing these daily habits will there be enough momentum and energy created to transform a negative environment into a positive one. Change, seen this way, is not a program your company goes through; it is a series of new decisions individuals make that are different than the old ones.

You make decisions every day. You decide whether you will drive straight to work, or whether you will stop for gas or coffee. You decide whether you will say "good morning" to people in the hall, or go straight to your office and get to work. You decide whether you will attend a meeting, support a project or avoid talking about a subject you know should be discussed. Each one of these decisions has an impact on the world. Each one creates (or avoids creating) an interaction that defines your relationship with someone.

Not every person in an organization must change for the environment to change; many will not. In fact, trying to change other people is a fool's errand; the only person you can change is yourself. What you can do, however, is change the way you interact with others. These changed interactions, at least in that moment, create a change in both people. Over time, these changes in daily interactions among individuals will change the organization.

These interactions and habits are created by decisions that you control. I hope that you decide to read this book. I hope that you decide after reading the book to change some of your daily habits and interactions with the people around you. I hope that others in your immediate network also decide to change some of their habits, based on your example. My most sincere hope is that these changes in interactions can create the momentum and energy needed to transform your organization. So, what is your decision?

Phillip B. Wilson
July 2003

Table of Contents
The Next 52 Weeks

Acknowledgements	v
Preface	vii
Table of Contents	xi
Chapter 1 - Introduction	1
The three common characteristics of companies recently petitioned by a union	2
What a union means to the management of an organization	5
Why union-free status is a poor indicator of an organization's skills	7
Symptoms of "at-risk" organizations and characteristics of leaders	10
How union "pre-emption" helps organizations achieve union-free status	15
You should avoid being overdrawn in your "Employee Relations Bank Account"	17
Chapter 2 - Learning to Think Like an Organizer - How Unions Organize Employees	18
How union organizing campaigns get started	19
Summary of the NLRB election process	21
Some of the common tactics used by organizers to persuade potential voters	22
The early warning signs of union organizing activity	24
The key campaign themes used by unions today	29
Chapter 3 - Motivations - Why Employees Choose to Be Union-Free	35
The three categories of union-free motivation: relevance, pragmatism and fear	37
Identifying the primary union-free motivation of your employees	43
Modifying your strategy based on the primary motivation of your employees	44
Chapter 4 - Third-Party Intervention, Vulnerability and Your Union Free Strategy	49
How do I figure my organization's Employment Misery Index?	51
How do I determine my organization's Regulatory Compliance Factor?	53
What items should be part of a successful employment practices audit?	54
How do I establish the Union Activity Profile for my area?	55
What impact does my company's size have on my vulnerability?	57
Chapter 5 - Employee Opinion Surveys - Your Employees Know Whether They Want a Union – Ask Them!	61
Why conducting an opinion survey after a union election is a good strategy	63
The types of opinion surveys you should consider	66
Whole system, appreciative inquiry, interviews and other survey methods	67
How to tabulate your survey information	72
Key considerations when constructing your survey	74
The best ways to communicate survey results to your employees	79
Legal issues regarding the conduct of opinion surveys	82
Chapter 6 - Supervisors – Foundation for Your Success	90
Why line-level supervision is the key to your success	91
The three reasons that supervisors so often form a weak foundation	92

What your supervisors and managers need to know about emotional intelligence — 93

How to change your promotion policies to ensure a successful supervisory team — 96

The key "soft-skills" to teach your supervisory team — 98

How to build accountability into your program — 101

Chapter 7 - Communication Strategies for Policies, Procedures, Benefits and Compensation — 105

Key principles: consistency, clarity, multiple channels — 106

How to <u>use</u> the grapevine instead of fighting it — 110

Testing your communication program — 111

Examples: polices, procedures, benefits and compensation issues — 115

Handling communication of bad news — 122

Chapter 8 - Employee Involvement – A True Win-Win — 128

When to use a team – and when <u>not</u> to use one — 129

Choosing the issue for a team — 131

Common causes for failed teams — 133

Examples of teams in action – safety and work conditions issues — 137

How to avoid the legal pitfalls that can be associated with the use of teams — 145

Chapter 9 - Recruiting, Hiring and Pre-Employment Screening — 151

How selection techniques can transform your employee relations environment — 152

Why an effective hiring program is the first step to employee retention — 155

The disadvantages of relying on "historical" data instead of present competency — 157

Strategies for creating narrow, objectively observable interviewing criteria — 158

The five keys to conducting a good interview — 160

Job simulations and hints on recruiting — 161

Chapter 10 - They're Hired, Now What? Orientation Programs — 166

Why the orientation process is critical — 167

Common mistakes made in the orientation process — 170

Strategies for planning new hire orientation — 170

Why you should consider lengthening the time of your new hire orientation — 173

Chapter 11 - Recognition and Motivation Strategies — 175

Why recognition and motivation is so difficult for most companies — 175

Low and no cost motivation programs — 178

Informal and formal recognition strategies — 179

Legal issues with implementing recognition or motivation programs — 181

Chapter 12 - Show Me the Money – How to Deal Effectively With the Challenges of Pay and Benefits — 184

How your exit interview process can identify key pay and benefit concerns — 185

Conducting a pay and benefit survey to attack external fairness issues — 188

Designing a pay and benefit plan to avoid internal fairness issues — 192

The disadvantages of keeping pay issues secret — 193

Legal issues regarding pay and benefit changes — 195

Chapter 13 - Performance Feedback That Works — 199

Are formal performance appraisals right for your organization? — 200

Evaluating whether your firm should tie performance appraisals to compensation   203

The three most common problems with appraisal systems and how to solve them   205

How to design an effective appraisal process   209

Tips to improve informal performance feedback   213

Chapter 14 - Dispute Resolution and Peer Review   215

"Pre-emption" of claims that normally go to third parties   218

Cost reductions that can be achieved through reliance on dispute resolution   219

Strategies to reduce the amount of time and energy your firm spends on disputes   222

Legal issues to consider when implementing a dispute resolution program   224

The main types of dispute resolution programs   229

Chapter 15 - Planning Your Fifty-Two Week Calendar   234

Steps to create a concrete vision of your ideal employee relations environment   236

Three key strategies for project planning   239

Importance of including employees in the planning and implementation process   244

Utilizing survey data to create your master plan   245

Chapter 16 - Where Do We Go From Here? Weeks 53 and Beyond   248

Some tips on how to keep your 52 Week program on track   249

Ideas for renewing your program in the years after your 52 Week program   254

Appendix 1 – Sample Opinions Survey Questions   256

Appendix 2 – Sample Survey Charts & Graphs   259

Appendix 3 – Sample Handbook and Policy Statements   260

Appendix 4 – Sample Exit Interview Form   268

Appendix 5 – Sample Next 52 Weeks Plan/Presentation   269

Index   271

About the Author, Publications   275

Chapter 1

Introduction

*"Only those who risk going too far will
ever know how far they can go."*
Anonymous

What You'll Learn In This Chapter
- ❑ The three common characteristics of companies recently petitioned by a union
- ❑ What a union means to the management of an organization
- ❑ Why union-free status is a poor indicator of an organization's employee relations skills
- ❑ The symptoms of "at-risk" organizations and characteristics of employee relations leaders
- ❑ How union "pre-emption" can help your organization achieve or maintain union-free status
- ❑ Why you should avoid being overdrawn in your "Employee Relations Bank Account"

What This Book Is ...And What It Isn't
Managing an employee relations environment is <u>hard</u>. It may not be rocket science, but it's the next hardest thing to get right. I do not believe anyone has figured out how to do it consistently. Since managing employee relations is harder than anything else a company does (unless, perhaps, you manufacture rockets) this probably explains why so few companies do it well.

The good news is that just about every company can significantly improve in this area by following some very simple steps. This book outlines those steps.

I write this book with two audiences in mind. The first is human resources and organization development professionals, interested in a unique view "from the trenches" about organization change in difficult environments. My second audience, and the one I write to most directly, is the leaders of organizations who have been involved in union organizing campaigns.

Characteristics of Companies Attacked by Unions

The bulk of my work is with companies after they have successfully defended themselves against a union organizing attempt. These companies have unique challenges and concerns that I address in this book. These companies rank among the worst at managing their employee relationships. They normally share three common characteristics:

- Employees lack trust or confidence in top management's ability to solve their problems, a problem worsened by a six week election campaign in which every decision made by management is examined under a microscope and picked apart by union organizers;
- Management has expended enormous effort communicating its position on unions, creating a void in communication after the campaign is over; and
- Expectations are created during the campaign and employees are waiting to see them fulfilled. These expectations are rarely explicit, and they are often unreasonable. Fair or not, management will be held to these expectations as employees judge whether they made a good decision in the voting booth.

Most companies are poorly prepared for winning a NLRB campaign. The natural reaction after winning a union election is to celebrate the victory, close the chapter and move on. This is understandable, given the huge expense and enormous loss of productivity that normally accompanies most campaigns. However, this reaction is very counterproductive; often this is the exact reaction union organizers count on.

If your company does not manage these three reactions properly, you are falling into a trap. Organizers rarely look at an organizing drive as a "one-shot" deal. Today unions are known to file second and even third petitions regularly. Any good organizer (no matter the results of the first election) can capitalize on the traits listed above, creating excellent campaign issues. The steps you take in the next six months will determine whether you will be vulnerable to another petition next year. A second petition within 3 years of an election results in a company loss over 80% of the time.

My hope is that this book will provide some helpful information and strategies for those interested in changing their employee relations environment. I also hope that it offers hope to those organizations that feel that their employee relations situation is hopeless. I provide some practical tools to use as a starting point in your change effort – a sketch to use as you begin to paint your own picture.

This book is not a comprehensive guide on the subject of organization change. I include at the end of this book some suggestions for additional reading that can help you add color and depth to your pallet. Your organization's environment is unique, and your change program will reflect that uniqueness. Yet I can tell you without reservation that you can successfully transform your employee relations environment. If you decide to try then I have accomplished my goal in writing this book.

This book describes a program I designed to attack the weaknesses most prevalent in these companies. So, is this an anti-union book? No. And I am not anti-union (no matter how many times I've been called a union buster). Many companies have a productive collective bargaining relationship with their employees, and some prefer to operate that way. And even these companies can profit from the lessons described in this book.

I do feel, however, that a company committed to operating union-free, that strives to create a workplace where employees do not feel the need for third party intervention, is a much better place to work than one that is not. I feel firmly that companies that lose union elections usually deserve it. I also believe that any company that follows the principles outlined in this book will never have to worry about being organized by a union.

What about companies that have never been threatened by a union and are already doing a good job in these areas? This book still offers a way to check the pulse of your company. I encourage all companies I work with, whether petitioned for a union election or not, to "think like an organizer." This method of thinking trains them to attack weaknesses as they arise. It is a logical, outcome-oriented method of continuous improvement that can dramatically improve your HR management system. Let's get started.

You Don't Want a Union, Right?

Most HR professionals, and almost all operations people (even officers of very large companies) answer this question in the affirmative without even thinking about it. About the only people I've met who really question this proposition are CFOs, usually for all the wrong reasons. Finance people are programmed to look only at how something hits the books or affects the bottom line – which never accounts for the financial impacts associated with an unhappy workforce.

I've sat through many meetings where the top finance officer argues for quite some time that "this union thing" won't hurt us and fighting it will just be expensive. Depending on the culture of that management team, the CFO might be right. If the company doesn't plan on correcting the issues that created an atmosphere ripe for organizing activity in the first place, the odds are that fighting it will be an expensive and, ultimately lost cause.

So why don't you want a union? The answers to this question will often depend on who you are. Good supervisors don't like unions because their jobs change from managers to contract administrators. (Bad supervisors, by definition, really couldn't care less). In the worst cases supervisors will spend the vast majority of their time dealing with minor administration issues instead of managing production. If they try to run things the old way, or if they get into a battle with the union or one of its officers, they will usually get the added pleasure of defending numerous grievances filed against them.

Operations managers don't want a union for all the reasons listed above. They become the ultimate contract administrator and usually have to resolve all the grievances filed. They spend an excessive amount (or most) of their time defending managerial actions of their supervisory team, often in front of outside parties who have no clue about the operation.

In addition, depending on the company, operations managers usually get to negotiate a contract every few years, with the possibility of work stoppages. In larger companies, they get to do this with the labor relations experts or lawyers shipped in to make sure they do a good job. Every major operational decision will include a significant discussion about how to get the union to sign off, and many good ideas will be simply tossed aside because of fears regarding implementation.

Human resources professionals have the most to lose when their workplace becomes unionized. Their jobs change dramatically (or they're fired and a "labor" person is brought in) when a union comes into the company. In addition to relearning the worst parts of their jobs – record keeping, benefits administration, hiring administration – there are the added headaches of contract negotiations, arbitrations and contract administration.

Furthermore, almost all of the positive employee relations opportunities are lost, because they are seen as a threat by the union (which has a vested interest in employees' distrust of management). The opportunities to make the workplace more cooperative are all but lost. I have heard stories about companies and unions working together, so I don't think it's impossible. On the other hand, I would say the vast majority of the time things become less cooperative and more adversarial.

Officers of companies that become unionized have to learn a new way of thinking about their businesses. Sometimes these people are also the operations managers (and even the human resources professionals) so they get all the headaches listed above and typically don't have enough hours in the day to worry about anything else. In larger companies, a unionized location adds an additional layer of bureaucracy on all operational and many financial decisions. Unionized locations are more rigid and often less productive than non-unionized ones.

Acquiring a union at one location makes your company much more vulnerable to organizing at other locations. (In fact, most unions today include neutrality and card-check recognition at non-union locations among their highest priority in contract negotiations at unionized plants.) Additionally, there is the obvious problem of potential work stoppages at unionized locations.

Financially, there are hundreds of additional expenses from legal fees and costs of in-house labor expertise to time lost in contract administration and the inability to deal fluidly with labor expense issues. (Temporary, part-time and overtime are life-and-death issues in unionized operations.) If you screw up a contract, you are usually stuck with it for three years and then have an enormous problem correcting past mistakes. There's a reason why unionized operations are typically valued at a significant discount in comparison to non-union ones.

Is There a Difference Between Union-free Companies and Unionized Ones?

In a broad sense, there is no difference between unionized companies and those labeled "union-free." You can have two identical companies making an identical product or offering an identical service and employing the same type of people, yet one may have a bargaining obligation and the other one may not.

It is incorrect to automatically assume that because a company has a bargaining obligation it is doing anything "wrong" or it is "worse" than a company without a union. In fact, the opposite is often true. There are thousands of companies out there that, although they don't have a legal bargaining obligation, have working conditions much worse than unionized companies. Unions of course would claim that this is *because* the companies are not unionized (also an overstatement in my opinion).

Many deluded CEOs and company owners believe that their union-free status is evidence that they are doing things right. Even worse is the owner who believes that because his employees voted in favor of the company in a representation election, he no longer has a union problem. This is a mistake made by managers of companies across the country. They believe that, because they are union-free, the company must be a great place to work. Union organizing drives are a symptom of a sick company and winning a union election, like getting an angioplasty, is not a cure. It protects you for a while, but if there is not a significant change in lifestyle, the patient may end up dead anyway.

It is instructive, then, to compare companies petitioned for representation against their will with companies having employees who have been approached by union organizers and turned them away. The former group of companies I refer to as "at-risk," meaning that, but for the grace of God, they probably would have a bargaining obligation. A tremendous number of companies in America fit into this category

Companies Who Get Organized Usually Deserve It

One can take the medical metaphor too far, but it is a good vehicle for discussing the "symptoms" of an at-risk business. Like the heart patient who refuses to follow his prescribed diet, at-risk companies that fail to react to and correct the symptoms of illness in their workforce are increasingly likely to have an attack.

It is funny how some company executives, particularly business owners who still run their own show, believe that they have an inalienable right to run their company the way they see fit and that no union is going to be able to take that away from them. It becomes a matter of principle to them: "I don't care what Section 7 says, and you and an army of lawyers ain't changing my mind -- we're not having any damn union here!"

I believe that companies that refuse to change their management style to respond to the problems evident in their workforce deserve to be unionized. Like physical health, if you refuse out of stubbornness, principle or even fear to respond to the symptoms, you should expect to pay the consequences.

Union organizers will scream from the highest mountain that employees have a right to organize. They are right. Of course they never mention the equal and opposite right to refrain from organizing. These people also refuse to acknowledge that this right is not the right of unions, but of employees. If employees don't want to join a union, they don't have to have one. Period.

By the same token, operating union-free is not a right. You can be virulently anti-union. You can hire union-busters and labor lawyers until you don't have any money left (not an uncommon occurrence), but if your employees want a union, they can get one. You can litigate and negotiate and commit all the unfair labor practices known to man, but if your employees *really* want a union, you can't stop it unless you close down your company. That, my friend, is the labor law version of a heart attack. You may somehow and miraculously get resuscitated, but basically you're dead.

Symptoms of "At-Risk" Companies
There are as many ideas on how to properly manage human resources as there are human resource professionals. However, over the years of working with companies that have been attacked by unions (and helping the ones who wanted to change their workplace immunize themselves from further organizing attempts) I have found several common symptoms endemic to at-risk companies. Of course, for each symptom there is a countervailing characteristic of "healthy" companies. The table below summarizes the most common symptoms and characteristics:

Symptom of "At-Risk" Company	Characteristic of Healthy Company
• Feeling that management fails to keep hourly employees informed	• Good communication of business issues; consistent feedback on job performance
• Poor complaint procedure – feeling that input is ignored	• Complaint and suggestion procedure in place; appeal

- Unfair application of policies and procedures

- Unfair promotion or advancement procedures

- Feeling that terminations are handled unfairly

- Poor working environment or conditions
- Uncertainty about future with the company

- Lack of training and development programs

- Pay and/or benefits below market levels – poorly communicated compensation and benefit plans

- Poor recruiting, pre-employment screening and new hire orientation process

- Poorly trained or incompetent front-line supervisors

---

process; consistent feedback
- Clearly communicated and fairly applied policies and procedures
- Clear, objective requirements for advancement; training and development available to prepare for advancement
- Unbiased review process for all terminations; appeal process
- Clean, comfortable and safe work environment
- Confidence in company's health and personal growth opportunities
- Variety of training opportunities; consistent dialogue on personal development
- Pay and benefits at or above market levels; well communicated compensation and benefit policies; clearly communicated and consistently applied salary administration
- Strong hiring and screening process; high effort during first several months of employment to ensure new hires are the right "fit"
- Effort made to promote individuals with best supervisory skills, not best technical skills; ongoing training and development of front-line supervisors

While no chart of this nature can capture all the weaknesses of "at-risk" organizations, these are the first things an organizer will look for when determining whether or not a company is a good target. They are, consequently, the first things you should look at when deciding where to begin your work to remain union-free.

What If We Already Have a Union?
This book is not only for companies who are without a bargaining obligation at the present time. All the principles discussed here can be applied in a unionized environment, so long as a few key points are remembered. First, many of the things I suggest in this book would be subject to a bargaining obligation and, therefore, should not be implemented without first offering to bargain with the union. Depending on your relationship with your union, this may mean you cannot accomplish everything you want. Of course, that's not a surprise to you if you have a union.

Even if your bargaining relationship is less than productive, there are still many areas where you can make improvements without bargaining. In particular, your pre-employment, orientation and supervisory development programs can normally be adjusted without bargaining. Second, you also need to consider your ultimate goal. If it is to one day create a work environment where employees will conclude that they no longer need union representation, you obviously want to avoid creating the impression that the union is driving the positive changes in the workplace (particularly if they are not). On the other hand, if your goal is to create a better bargaining relationship, you will want to join with the union in implementing these changes.

Obviously these are strategic issues well beyond the scope of this text. The key point here is that unionized and non-union operations are encouraged to consider implementing as many of the applicable aspects of this program as possible. The mere fact that a bargaining obligation exists does not mean that a company cannot transform itself into an employee relations leader.

What's the Secret?

People often ask me, "What is the secret to maintaining union-free status?" I usually reply, as taught by my mentor Dick Wessels, "there are no silver bullets in labor law." If there is any "secret" at all, it is that you must be vigilant in wanting to make your workplace as good a place to work as possible. It requires constant effort, and small mistakes can have enormous impact.

There are two theories on avoiding third party intervention. The first is to eliminate its source, or as I like to refer to it "cutting the head off the dragon." This approach is attractive to clients because it is the quick fix. You've heard of the situation where that horribly disgruntled employee finally leaves, usually involuntarily, and it's like a cloud has been lifted from the workplace. The supposed success of this approach (by itself), like dragons, is a myth.

Client Story
Why "Cutting the Head Off the Dragon" is Not Enough

A longtime client recently called us on the work in his case. The company fought three organizing campaigns back to back, and after winning the third, we were asked to help turn things around. The last campaign, as one might imagine, was horrible. Soon after we began working with the company, we witnessed one of the most incredible displays of insubordination from an employee ever seen/experienced. (He was also quite outspoken in favor of the union.) This employee accosted the owner of the plant and nearly assaulted him.

A week or two later during a conference call, I learned that not only was the employee still with the company, but he did not even suffer disciplinary action for the incident Why? He was the number one union supporter and had already filed many unfair labor practice charges over the prior campaigns. I was dumbfounded. I asked why the company decided to let this guy run the plant, and why they had even hired us at all. After hearing about legal fees and how unfair the NLRB is on discharge cases (both entirely true) I had heard enough. "Either fire him, or fire us," I said.

The client saw this as the reason for our success. I did not. Firing an employee whom you have just cause to fire is not a great act of courage – it is just common sense. The fear of unfair labor practice charges being filed during union campaigns, when they are filed in virtually every discharge situation no matter how egregious, is a weak excuse to fail to do the right thing. This employee's union sympathy was totally irrelevant. He was one of nearly a hundred union supporters, and not even the most vocal. However, he was the only employee who was disrespectful and openly hostile to all management. This employee believed he was untouchable – and his co-workers knew it. So he spent his workday making every other employee in the company miserable. He was a cancer.

Yet firing this employee was only a small first step. The action created an environment in which the company could get the benefit of the doubt – but only that. Consistent, measured and public acts over the course of months were needed to turn this workforce around. Solving the problems involved supervisory

training, implementation of a variety of positive programs for employees, and a bunch of hard work.

Ultimately, these employees determined that it was time to give the company a chance. Does this mean a union is now an impossibility there? Absolutely not. Did terminating this one employee "win" the case? No way. Consistent attention to the employees of this company will keep the company union-free forever. Failure to continue the lessons learned will lead to election number four – and near-certain defeat.

The second theory is called "substitution" by unions, but I like to call it "preemption." This approach recognizes that in most workplaces where third-party intervention is a risk, the "dragon" is more like the Hydra from ancient mythology – you cut off its head and it just keeps coming back. This is the usual situation and the quick fix doesn't work. Although things might get better for a while, the root causes of the problem do not go away with the fired employee. So after a little while a new dragon head appears, usually more fierce than the last. And if you play with dragons long enough (OK, OK, I'll stop with the dragon metaphor after this) you're going to get burnt.

Third-party intervention, whether by unions, government agencies or other employee representatives, is a response to something that has gone wrong. I've seen it referred to recently as the "toxic workplace," which is an apt description for many of the companies in which we are asked to get involved. Unfortunately, there's no magic elixir that will clean up a toxic workplace. Sure, a supervisor or manager here or there may need to go, but the problems in these workplaces are almost always deeper than that.

In order to effectively eliminate the need and/or threat of third- party intervention, it is important to remember why employees seek it in the first place. Employees turn to third parties when they feel
- a problem or issue is too big to handle on their own;
- the third party will get them more or get them a better outcome than they can on their own; or
- the third party somehow adds more credibility to their problem or issue.

Any strategy to eliminate the threat of third-party intervention must attack each of these three motivations.

Unions like to refer to "substitution" because it implies that everyone wants what they've got (although they might "settle" for a substitute). I refer to it as preemption, like when the federal government passes a law that prevents other actions by state or local governments. Third-party preemption occurs when a company takes actions in an area that limits a third party's ability to act in that same area.

The key is to focus your third party preemption strategies on the three areas described above – helping employees deal with all problems (especially the "big" ones); convincing employees that they can get as much or more for themselves without turning to third parties; and helping them believe that there is no additional credibility gained by turning to a third party. This framework will help clean up the underlying problems that lead to interventions and, if or when they do occur, make those interventions less costly.

I often see managers get extremely frustrated when they begin the transformation into an employee relations leader. They feel like their hard work is totally unappreciated. There is nothing more frustrating than to have made a commitment in your own mind to really want to solicit employee opinion, only to hear a collective yawn in response. A commitment such as this requires incredible patience. Employees in a company that has consistently failed to listen have been trained not to talk. They must be retrained, and this process takes time. Trust, which is what all this comes down to in the end, is something that is earned over time.

An example that I find compelling is Steven Covey's "emotional bank account." Covey believes that we should look at our personal relationships like mini bank accounts, in which emotional deposits and withdrawals are made. If you act like a jerk to someone, you've made a withdrawal. If you are nice, you've made a deposit. Companies are the same way – they have what I call an Employee Relations Bank Account. Those that have consistently failed in their employee relations practices are probably overdrawn in their accounts with their employees. It will take a significant number of deposits before these businesses will begin to see results.

So the secret is to commit to change and to stick to your plan, even if it looks like nobody else is with you. Experience shows that the methods/philosophies suggested here are the best way to manage your employee relations. You will get resistance – any change, no matter how beneficial in the end, is usually met with resistance at first. The key is to meet the resistance head-on, stay vigilant and know that one day the resistance will turn into cooperative effort aimed toward goals and a better way to get the job done.

Chapter 2

Learning to Think Like an Organizer - How Unions Organize Employees

"What else can you expect with peace running wild all over the place? You know what the trouble is with peace? No organization."
Bertolt Brecht, Mother Courage and Her Children

What You'll Learn In This Chapter
- ❑ How union organizing campaigns get started
- ❑ Summary of the NLRB election process
- ❑ Some of the common tactics used by organizers to persuade potential voters
- ❑ The early warning signs of union organizing activity
- ❑ The key campaign themes used by unions today

For companies that have undergone a union organizing effort, one key to this program is to teach managers to think like organizers. If you appreciate how unions attack companies, you can better defend against those attacks. More important, if you have already identified and improved the areas organizers focus on to gain support, organizers will have a tough time finding issues needed to get a campaign to take hold. If the ground is barren, the organizer will look elsewhere to plant.

There are three things you need to do in order to start "thinking like an organizer." First, you must thoroughly understand how unions organize workers. Second, you should be aware of the early warning signs of union organizing. Third, you must learn the themes and tactics used by today's organizers. If you fully understand these areas, you will be far ahead of the game as you plan your own union-prevention strategy.

How Unions Organize Employees

Union organizing is not a mystery. Contrary to what many practitioners preach, unions do have a product to sell. It is called "a better future." The better they do the job of convincing potential members that they can deliver this product, the more likely they are to win a union-organizing election. Like any other election campaign, unions organize employees using typical grassroots campaign strategies. They visit homes. They pass out campaign literature. They make speeches and hold rallies. Sometimes they even advertise. Sure, unions will also engage in economic pressure tactics against an employer (see *The Jagged Edge* at the end of this chapter), but the only way unions have any hope of winning is by convincing a majority of employees in an appropriate unit that they will have a better future organized than not.

I had the pleasure of listening to a speech given by Richard Bensinger a couple of years ago. Bensinger was the very first head of organizing for the AFL-CIO. He left that post after some undisclosed conflicts with the AFL-CIO leadership. Although he never made the admission, my feeling while listening to him speak was that he was just too honest with the leadership to remain politically capable of doing his job. It probably did not take long for Bensinger to burn a lot of bridges by naming the heads of unions who were more interested in waiting to collect a pension than expanding their membership. He seemed to hold union leaders to organizing standards they are not prepared to attain. Nevertheless, he also appeared to be a man of great integrity and vision.

Bensinger is very disappointed in the labor movement, particularly with regard to organizing. His comments, I feel, are equally applicable to management. Bensinger believes that the labor law is unfairly tilted toward management, and has some compelling arguments in his favor. (We probably would still have a Whig Party president if, after every presidential election, you could prevent the winner from taking office by filing objections to the conduct of the election – just look at the 2000 presidential race!) But, he claims that unions put too much blame on things like the labor law.

Bensinger argues that unions can continue to lobby for card-check recognition and other rules to ease organizing, but that until unions create a mass appeal to the idea of being organized, they will never succeed. While he supports ideas like card-check recognition and streamlined voting procedures, Bensinger also says that if the union doesn't have a solid majority, it should walk away. Although we approach the issue from opposite ends of the spectrum, I couldn't agree with the conclusion more.

Companies can also complain about the law favoring unions (There are certainly some compelling arguments on this side as well) and lobby as hard as they want against changes that make organizing easier. But if they don't ensure that their employees see no need for third party representation, all the lobbying and rules changes are useless.

One thing is certain. No matter which way the campaign gets started, a union can only be successful if there are a substantial number of employees who feel that union representation is in their best interest. Without that basic element, none of the tactics can ultimately· succeed. By the same token, the union's worst-run organizing campaign will succeed where the employees of a company see no other way to protect their futures.

How Do Organizing Campaigns Get Started?
There are three primary ways an organizing campaign gets started. First, and most common, is when an employee or group of employees at a company get fed up and contact the union. The second type of campaign is one where the union targets a company, usually as part of an industry or community campaign strategy. The union will try to contact employees at target companies and attempt to start organizing activity even if there was no initial call for help. Sometimes they will "Salt" an employer, sending a union organizer in to apply for a job with the intent that, if hired, that individual will start an organizing campaign.

The third type of organizing campaign is the corporate campaign. This campaign is directed at top management and even corporate board members. It is intended to embarrass a company, usually one that is in the public limelight, into recognizing the union. Campaigns that start under methods one and two can also use corporate campaign tactics. Other corporate campaigns are intended to create financial problems for an unorganized competitor or to create competitive advantages for unionized companies in the same industry.

A Quick Summary of the Process

There are several things that must occur before a union can be voted in as a collective bargaining representative.[1]   First, they have to make a valid "showing of interest."   This is usually done through authorization cards. Unions can either be certified as a bargaining representative through an election conducted by the National Labor Relations Board (NLRB), or an employer can voluntarily recognize a union as the bargaining representative of its employees. In either event, the union is required to show, whether through ballots cast or (in the case of voluntary recognition) through authorization cards or a petition, that the majority of employees wish to be represented.

Most companies refuse to voluntarily recognize the union, which means the union must file a petition with the NLRB for an election. Once a petition is filed, there is about a one-month period during which a campaign is held. If employees are convinced that unionization is not in their best interest and vote against representation, there is a one-year period during which a union cannot petition for an election in that same unit. After that period, the process can start again. (Often the card-signing process and campaigning continue during the one-year "insulated" period, which is allowed.)

---

[1] I assume that most readers of this book are familiar with how the organizing process works. Although I summarize that process briefly here, a full description is beyond the scope of this text. Note that this is only a summary, and there are many details not covered. For a full treatment, refer to Wilson, *Total Victory: The Complete Management Guide to a Successful NLRB Representation Election, 2d Edition.* (Labor Relations Institute 1997).

Information-Gathering – the Union's "Secret" Weapon

When a union is first approached to organize a company (if "called in" by employees) or when the union is deciding to organize a company from the outside, they will engage in an information-collecting process. This process must be fully understood if you are serious about maintaining your union-free status. Union organizers want to know as much as possible about a target company before beginning a campaign. They will study every aspect of the business in an effort to define campaign issues, learn weaknesses of the company, and customize general themes to the particular facts of the target.

This information-collecting process was described at length in a textbook for union organizers titled *A Troublemakers Handbook*. That book contains an interview with Richard Leonard, an organizer for the Oil, Chemical and Atomic Workers Union, who explains how he begins gathering information for an effective campaign. Leonard looks at sources such as a company's 10-K and annual financial reports to get financial data. He researches articles from newspapers and magazines. He uses search services to find out who the major shareholders and the company insiders are, and if there are any major institutional investors.

Leonard also conducts group interviews with employees whenever possible. He states, "the thing that empowers workers is knowledge. What we do is based on the notion that the workers know as much if not more about the company than management does, at least at that location. If you can collect this knowledge, it can work miracles. I've seen it happen over and over again."[2]

I have seen the 3-ring binders union organizers create during major organizing drives. They're chock full of company information, and they're impressive. These guys can sit down with an hourly employee, flip open a slick binder full of newspaper articles touting the company and financial reports showing numbers most hourly workers can't even comprehend, and soon that employee is very upset. They will include copies of employee handbook statements that are favorable to the union (especially statements on "at-will" employment and termination). They will show contracts at other workplaces where employees make more money. Their agenda is very much a sales process, and organizers are very good at selling the program.

After spending time talking with employees and gathering information, union organizers will be able to target the campaign to the specific issues relevant to that particular work force. Organizers will know that the attendance policy isn't enforced fairly across departments or that the supervisor on second shift is a real jerk. They will begin to package the sales pitch to account for these known problems. They will "prove" how much money the company is making (whether true or not) and tell prospective members they need to get their share. This propaganda is very difficult to counter.

Therefore, when thinking like an organizer, your first job is to gather this same information. The company, of course, is in a much better position to collect it.

---

[2] Dan LaBotz, *A Troublemaker's Handbook*, (Labor Notes, 1991) p. 132.

The problem is that most companies never look at these things through the eyes of an organizer. The process of gathering this information is enlightening and puts your company in a position of strength when it comes to responding to organizing. If you don't gather this information, you are wide open to invasion when the organizer comes knocking.

Recognizing the Early Warning Signs

The purpose of thinking like an organizer is to be prepared for organizing before it occurs. Once your company has integrated the concepts outlined in this book into your employee relations plan, most organizing activity will fall on deaf ears. Yet, while the purpose of THE NEXT 52 WEEKS™ program is to protect your company from organizing activity altogether, there is no way to eliminate the possibility of card-signing activity.

Unions are increasingly sophisticated in their handling of "pre-petition" campaigning, and many companies are taken completely by surprise when a petition is filed. They shouldn't be. I don't know how many times I have heard companies who were petitioned look back (hindsight is 20/20 after all) and remember an incident and say, "How could we be so blind? I should have known right then that we were being organized." There are many signs that organizing activity is occurring in a workplace; you just have to pay attention to them.

You should train yourself and your managers and supervisors to always be on the lookout for potential activity. This way, you are not taken by surprise, and you can often respond to potential problems before a possibility exists/arises for groundswell support. The list below outlines my "Top Ten" early warning signs of organizing activity. Next to each warning sign, I outline how each sign should be interpreted.

- *Union Authorization Cards – Fliers*: This probably shouldn't count as an "early" warning sign. If you see authorization cards or leaflets, you have an organizing campaign on your hands. Contact your labor attorney immediately and get your counter-organizing campaign started.
- *Strangers Meeting with Employees Near the Company*: Again, a not too "early" sign. I hope you would be aware of organizing activity before business agents show up at your property – they usually don't get this public unless they are very close to getting enough cards to file a petition or are having difficulty meeting with people outside of work. Unions don't want management to learn about the activity until they are ready to file their petition.
- *Rumors of Cardsigning, Meetings or Other Union Activity*: This is a common early warning sign. As the union attempts to expand support outside of its core group of supporters, it will inevitably have to approach people without being able to predict where they stand on the issue. If union workers approach a strong company supporter, this will often be communicated to a supervisor. Sometimes an observant (or lucky) supervisor will overhear a conversation. This sign requires immediate response.
- *Open Talk About Unions, Pro-Union Slogans as Graffiti*: This early warning sign does not necessarily mean that organizing activity is occurring. In every large work force there always seems to be a few people who, in

response to any work problem, will cry, "If we had a union here you wouldn't be able to get away with that." Same thing goes for graffiti. (But look on the bright side - at least "Union Yes!" takes less time to clean up than "Here I sit all broken-hearted..."). You obviously have to consider the source. However, if these comments or graffiti seem to be occurring more frequently than normal, you should certainly start looking for other early warning signs.

- *Employees Compiling Contact Information on Co-workers*: The union's preferred method of early campaigning is phone calls and home visits away from the workplace. In order to do this, however, organizers have to collect phone numbers and addresses. They will enlist inside organizers for this information. Most companies have policies against this sort of activity, as well they should. If you catch someone engaging in this subversive activity that employee should be disciplined under the policy, and you should start looking for some of the other warning signs. Do not try to find out directly from the individual whether he or she was compiling the information for union organizing purposes – this creates potential unfair labor practice liability and could prevent you from enforcing your policy.
- *Increased Complaints – "Grievances" About "Past Practice"*: Complaints certainly do not always mean organizing activity is occurring, but an unusual increase in the number or frequency of complaints often corresponds with organizing activity. You should particularly pay attention to the way the complaints are worded. If words like

"grievance," "past practice," "arbitration" or other terms usually found in labor contracts are being used, the likelihood is that someone with a union background is encouraging the complaints.

- *Unusual Interest in Company Policy, Handbooks:* An unusual increase in the number of requests for employee handbooks or copies of policies can also be a signal of organizing activity. Union organizers want to have copies of these documents and will ask employees for copies of their employee handbook or policy manuals.

- *Changes in Attitude, Silent Treatment of Managers:* Union organizers begin their campaigns by breeding mistrust of management. They will tell employees not to talk to supervisors or managers. Employees also fear that if management learns of their organizing activity they will be terminated. Employees who may have earlier had good relationships with a manager may now change their attitude or stop communicating. This is one of the more common warning signs, not just of organizing activity, but also of other potential problems (alcohol or drug problems, for example). These changes should be thoroughly investigated when they occur.

- *New Leaders – Unusual Groupings of Employees:* Employees who lead organizing campaigns are not typically high performers. Employees who want the "protection" they think a union provides are usually low performers. These employees normally are not considered leaders in the workforce. (Of course, there are exceptions to the rule, and an employee has to possess some leadership capacity to get a campaign going.) If employees with this profile suddenly take a leadership role or gain a following among employees who did not spend much time with them before, this can be a sign of organizing activity.

- *Union Activity in the Community:* Another important signal that should alert you to be on the lookout for organizing activity is an increase in organizing in your community, especially at a competitor or business in close proximity to your location. Unions will often focus on a particular industry and if they are organizing one business in an area, they also will try to generate interest at other businesses in the area.

Today's Key Issues and Campaign Themes

Another important part of thinking like an organizer is to know and understand the themes and language organizers use to persuade employees to join a union. There are a number of common themes used in almost all campaigns today. It is important to be able to respond to these issues and, more important, to educate your employees regarding them.

One major theme today is that of wage inequality. Unions always promise wage and benefit increases as part of their sales pitch to employees. In addition to making these promises, which employees may or may not believe, unions also make a broader social argument about distribution of wealth. Union organizers point to statistics showing the increased gap between the highest paid and lowest paid members of the workforce.

Unions also highlight the large compensation packages of corporate leaders and point to corporate profits to make their claim. The AFL-CIO sponsors a popular Web page called "CEO Pay Watch" (http://www.aflcio.org) that tracks the compensation of several major CEOs. They even have a board game that further illustrates the point. This issue resonates with many employees today.

A second important theme today is workplace democracy. Unions promise to give employees a voice in their workplace. Union organizers make employees believe that, with a union, they will be able to change the things they don't like about their workplace. This theme is compelling and promises to give power to those who may feel powerless.

Another theme used in campaigns today is that of dignity and justice. A now-famous industry campaign by the Service Employees Union is "Justice for Janitors," and is focused on organizing housekeeping, maintenance and janitorial departments in companies across the country. Unions convince employees who may feel discriminated against or treated unfairly that the union can prevent this treatment. And this ploy works. The chart below shows how union win rates increase when dignity and fairness issues are a major issue.

1986-87 NLRB Elections[3]

UNION TACTIC	Sample Proportion or mean	Proportion or mean for wins	Percentage win rate*
70% or more employees	.53	.57	.46 (.39)

[3] Kate Bronfenbrenner and Tom Juravich, "It Takes More Than House Calls: Organizing to Win with a Comprehensive Union-Building Strategy," *Organizing to Win: New Research on Union Strategies* (Cornell University Press, 1998), p. 23.

surveyed one-on-one			
Bargaining committee created before election	.15	.23	.64 (.39)
Solidarity days used	.12	.15	.53 (.41)
Union held rallies	.03	.04	.50 (.42)
Union held job actions	.02	.05	.10 (.41)
Community-labor coalitions used	.16	.19	.50 (.41)
Union used media	.11	.14	.52 (.41)
Dignity, fairness primary issues	.27	.36	.56 (.37)
Total number rank-and-file tactics used	2.12	2.69	NA

*Number in parentheses is the percentage win rate when the tactic or characteristic did not occur

Richard Leonard again explains the strategy: "In all such newsletters or other communications – such as articles in local newspapers that you clip and mail – it's important for the union to present itself as commanding the high ground. This means that the company is allowed ownership of the goals of profit and personal ambition, greed, etc., while the union appropriates the goals of quality, customer satisfaction, productivity, fairness, equitable social cost accounting, etc."[4]

Employers who wish to remain union-free need to be aware of these common themes and co-opt them as part of their own communication strategy. When employees are approached by a union organizer with these issues, they should have an immediate reaction of, "I don't need a union for that – my company already does it." If you accomplish this, you will never have an organizing problem.

---

[4] Dan LaBotz, *A Troublemaker's Handbook*, (Labor Notes, 1991) p. 135.

The Jagged Edge – What's New In Organizing

Unions are focusing on organizing. For years critics have stated that this is necessary due to the huge drop in union membership during the past few decades. Unions have talked about the need to organize for years, but the talk produced little tangible evidence of results. Even well-publicized programs like "union-summer" created lots of fanfare, but very few new union members.

However, the statistics now indicate that unions are beginning to do a better job in this area. Their winning percentage in organizing elections is going up. More important, the number of members that unions have gained in those elections has increased. Union workers are not filing as many petitions as in years past, but they appear to be picking their targets better.

A significant amount of attention is being paid to organizing at the very highest ranks of various AFL-CIO unions. One of the top posts in this organization is the Director of Organizing. "Old-school" union leaders are being forced out or replaced (Lane Kirkland by John Sweeney, the late Edward Hanley by John W. Wilhelm). The replacements are much more highly motivated organizers.

A terrific amount of work still needs to be done in order to weed out some of the old school thinking in unions across the country, but there is certainly more being said and done about organizing now than in recent memory. The AFL-CIO has also asked that its member unions pledge a minimum of 10% of assets to organizing activities.

Unions are leveraging community-based contacts to assist with organizing efforts. A variety of new and bold techniques are gaining popularity. A few are listed below, with a brief description of how each operates:

- Corporate Campaigns – Unions are taking on large targets and using national resources to attack them. They are using corporate campaign tactics previously used in strike situations to organize large corporate employers. Unions now pressure corporate board members and executives, personalize the campaigns, and employ legal guerilla warfare tactics and other strategies against them. Some of the best current examples of this tactic are the sweatshop campaigns against Wal-Mart and K-Mart stores by UNITE and the more direct campaigns against health care giants like Kaiser Permanente, Catholic Healthcare and Genesis.
- Political and Religious Leaders – Unions today do not hesitate to enlist the support of political and religious leaders in organizing campaigns. In several recent cases, local priests and ministers have been enlisted to convince employees to join a union. Organizing meetings are held in churches and churches distribute handouts listing biblical quotations "encouraging" organizing activities.
- "Virtual" Organizing – Several recent campaigns have occurred largely over the Internet. Borders Books, Microsoft and Intel have all fought (and continue to fight) Internet-based campaigns intended to increase support for unions. The AFL-CIO is using its Web page expertly in trying to organize new workers, and many affiliated unions (USW, UAW, IBT and SEIU to name just a few) are doing the same.

- Collective Bargaining as a Civil Right – this is a prevalent theme in leftist literature today and is increasingly common rhetoric in contemporary political discourse and in organizing campaigns. Using the same themes and arguments of civil rights leaders of the 1960s, labor leaders hope to usher in a new era of rights founded on the freedom to organize and bargain collectively.
- Class Warfare – One of the more popular themes for union organizers today is the gap between rich and poor in the United States. The CEO Paywatch, discussed earlier, is a very popular Internet site publicizing the large salaries of today's top corporate officials. It paints a very ugly picture of corporate greed. Equal pay is another powerful issue intended to motivate women, who today make up the majority of wage earners in the American workforce.

These are a few of the themes and tactics targeted companies must be prepared to respond to over the coming years. Unions are desperate to increase their memberships and remain very powerful organizations. Unions have proven again and again that, when pushed, they can bring political, social and economic power to bear to accomplish their goals. For an employer to remain union-free over the long haul, it is critical to remember these facts and to employ strategies that respond to the unions' strength.

Chapter 3

Motivations - Why Employees Choose to Be Union-Free

"Here choose I. Joy be the consequence!"
William Shakespeare, The Merchant of Venice

What You'll Learn In This Chapter
- ❏ The three categories of union-free motivation: relevance, pragmatism and fear
- ❏ Identifying the primary union-free motivation of your current group of employees
- ❏ How the primary motivation impacts your employee relations efforts
- ❏ Modifying your strategy based on the primary union-free motivation of your employees

If Employees Want a Union, They'll Get One.
There are many freedoms taken for granted in our country and many more privileges assumed. Unions claim that the right to organize a union, for example, is a civil right on an equal level with the right to be free from racial or sexual discrimination. On the other hand, many employers feel they have a right to operate their business as they see fit -- without a union.

I don't know how many times I have heard a client, after he or she first learns of organizing activity, calmly declare, "We won't be having a union here." It is as if to say that by willing it away, the union will be gone. If only the solution were that simple. The fact is that, legally, if a majority of employees in any company want a union and are willing to go through the proper procedure, they will get one. Period.

As ridiculous as the recent civil rights rhetoric from the house of labor might be, one thing is certain -- a protected right exists for employees to organize a union. Unlike other civil rights (i.e., rights based on characteristics for which an individual has no choice like race, gender or national origin), employees also have a right to refrain from organizing activity. Therefore, labor's call for the supremacy of the right to organize is misguided -- it ignores the right of others (the majority, in fact) to refrain from organizing. Nevertheless, the employer who wishes to remain union-free must recognize the nature of the rights granted to employees under the NLRA.

Many employers, especially smaller companies that may have begun as family businesses or closely held organizations, refuse to understand the concept that employees have the right to bargain collectively over wages, hours and working conditions. The fact that a person can build a successful business without any interference whatsoever and then, after one simple vote, suddenly have to negotiate with an outside third party seems un-American. Some company owners go so far as to close down their businesses to avoid giving up control over these issues.

The simple fact remains that an employer who plans to remain in business and remain union-free can only do so with the consent of the individuals employed by the organization. I spend a significant portion of my first hours with clients making sure they internalize this concept. I want them to understand they are not in control of this situation. While this concept is often difficult for business owners to grasp, it is fundamental to an understanding of how to remain union-free. If you understand that the decision to operate union-free is not yours alone, but ultimately resides in the hands of the individuals who work for you, your strategy will begin to gain clarity.

Relevance, Pragmatism and Fear

It is imperative to gain the support of your employees. The majority of them must believe that they prefer working directly with you rather than through an outside bargaining agent. Employees will reach this conclusion for any number of reasons. This nearly infinite number of motivations can be separated, however, into three broad categories: relevance, pragmatism and fear. These categories are summarized below, ranging from the most preferable motivation to the least preferable:

3 Categories of Union-Free Motivation

Relevance – These employees like their current work environment, are loyal to the current leadership, and are internally motivated to continue representing themselves as individuals in the workplace. It is virtually impossible to convince this group to seek unionization as an alternative.

Pragmatism – While employees in this environment may not love their current employer, they have examined the facts and do not want to pay for representation they can provide for themselves or feel will be ineffective. These employees choose the devil they know versus the one they don't.

Fear – These employees are the easiest to organize. They choose to remain unorganized due to either implicit or, worse, explicit threats regarding their job security, the company's security or the outcome of negotiations. Groups of employees with this motivation have little trust of management and are difficult to turn around.

It is important to recognize that a workforce may contain groups of employees with each of these motivations (or even individuals with more than one motivation) i.e., some may generally feel that a union is not relevant to them, but others may not consider unionization because they fear conflict in the workplace.

How Union-free Motivation Affects Your Plan

Whatever the myriad reasons your employees have for remaining union-free, there is normally one overriding motivation. As an employer you must understand this motivation, which will drive any attempt to re-work your employee relations strategy. Let's look at the three categories of motivations in greater detail in order to identify how different motivations will alter your approach to re-tooling your employee relations program.

Fear

Fear is the least effective motivation. Unscrupulous or simply unsophisticated employers use this approach during the organizing campaign process, but it is also a prevalent tactic among employers who have not experienced organizing problems. Unions rail against this approach and frequently point to employer tactics in this category as the primary reason for loss of union density in recent years -- even though unions frequently use fear and intimidation techniques during their organizing activities.

Experience teaches, however, that employers who rely on fear as a primary motivational tool are the most likely to lose an organizing campaign. This occurs for two reasons. First, as alluded to previously, unions are very effective at turning fear of employer tactics into reasons for choosing a union. An employer who fires employees or threatens to close down an operation during an organizing campaign is a sitting duck when it comes to organizing success for unions. Not only do these tactics create a huge number of issues from which employees feel they need protection, but they also create potential unfair labor practice liability. These charges, if proven egregious enough, can lead to a legal order to bargain with the union.

Second, fear can only motivate individuals for limited periods -- employees become numb to it. Eventually, good employees (particularly in today's highly competitive employment environment) will leave an employer who relies on fear. They will seek out employment in environments that are less stressful. Employers who rely on fear are not employers of choice and will eventually be left with lower-skilled and unmotivated employees (those who may feel they are unemployable, for example) while competitors gain higher-caliber workers. This scenario is not a recipe for long-term business success. As today's focus on work/family balance suggests, maintaining a healthy work environment is a key method of attracting talent. In today's increasingly knowledge-based economy, the company with the most talent wins.

The High Road

The Service Employees International Union (SEIU) recently issued a new manual for its health care organizers titled *"The High Road: A Winning Strategy for Managing Conflict and Communicating Effectively in Hospital Worker Organizing Campaigns."* The manual is based on a two-year study of experimental approaches to organizing hospital units. The study included opinion polls and focus groups of hospital workers. The study reached four conclusions:

- Decisions made by hospital workers to join a union are primarily made for pragmatic reasons;
- Hospital workers' concerns about conflict outweigh their desire for a voice in at their hospital;
- The most effective strategy for unions, even in hospitals where employer opposition is intense, is to stay on the high road with a positive campaign; and
- The methods that organizers use to manage conflicts in an organizing campaign can dramatically influence the outcome.

The lessons the SEIU learned provide some important lessons for management as well.

First, the tried and true tactic that organizations use when attacked by unions is fear. Companies often base a campaign on the alarming issues of strikes, violence, trials and a number of other "hot button" issues. These issues can turn fence-sitters into company supporters or, at least, reduce their support for the union. Even when not relying on these concerns, companies will focus on the conflict injected into the workplace by the union, driving a wedge between employees and management. The SEIU found that the vast majority of the time employers have plenty of evidence to point out this conflict.

Second, the decision to vote for or against unionization is not visceral, but pragmatic. This is a critical lesson. Instilling fear only works to the extent that the target is affected in a way that enforces your position. The SEIU found that employees weighed fear of unionization against the perceived advantages of the union. By downplaying this fear and refusing to inject additional anxiety into the campaign, the SEIU learned that employees are more likely to weigh the alternatives fairly. The SEIU also learned that by taking the high road they defuse some of the fear injected by employers, thereby exposing it for the tactical ploy it often is.

Stressing the possibility of confrontations and conflict during the campaign, the SEIU found, can be effective for management, but has its costs. The SEIU learned that by taking the high road (moving from fear to pragmatism) they could defuse the conflict often present during a union campaign. The SEIU teaches organizers to respond to conflict by explaining that it is just an unfortunate tactic used by employers and it will go away once the election is won. By appealing to the pragmatic side and helping to defuse conflict (not adding to it, and not giving management excuses to escalate the conflict), the union gains the upper hand during the campaign. Unions, like employers, would ultimately like to shift from the pragmatic motivation to one of relevance.

Pragmatism

This motivation is not nearly as problematic as fear. In fact, when we assist a company that has primarily driven its union-free strategy through instilling fear (especially if the fear strategy has failed and the employees are openly seeking a union), we will often turn to pragmatism as our primary communication model. Nevertheless, in the long run this strategy is also unsustainable.

Pragmatism motivates employees to remain union-free by means of logic. Explaining the disadvantages of collective bargaining, the risks associated with strikes or recounting examples of employees who were failed by their union are effective strategies. These appeals can be very persuasive with workers – very few employees who look at the facts objectively will decide that unionization is desirable.

Pragmatic appeals, however, particularly after an extended period of time, begin to lose their effectiveness and eventually fail. An employer who relies only on pointing out the negatives of unions, but fails to respond to internal problems, does not earn the trust of its employees. Unions can return the favor, reminding employees of the number of grievances and complaints they have and promising to resolve them. If these grievances and complaints have occurred over a period of time during which the company has made empty promises to resolve them, the union's pragmatism can be very persuasive.

For this reason, employers faced with second union elections lose over 80% of the time. The "give us another chance" campaign is just not that persuasive. An employer who fails to respond to employee concerns in effect says, "We don't care what you think." Employees tend to respond in kind.

Relevance
This strategy is by far the most effective and sustainable of the three. An employer whose employees honestly feel that their work environment is fulfilling and their jobs are challenging, rewarding and important will not seek unionization and will reject the notion out of hand when it is proposed. Employees in this environment simply cannot imagine what a union could contribute to their work environment. This work environment is "inoculated" in a sense, because it is not fertile ground for organizing activity.

Operating Union Free is Not an Accident

Before deciding on a direction to take with an employee relations strategy, you must not only know what issues your employees confront, but also what motivates them. If your employees are primarily motivated by fear, the first step is building trust between management and co-workers. If pragmatism is the prime motivator, the first step is moving past this calculated support for the company to internal motivation. This motivation will manifest itself in support for the company. If relevance is the primary motivation of your employees (in which case there is probably little current fear of union activity), then the key is to maintain those aspects of the employment environment that create this internal motivation.

This sounds good, but how does it work in practice? Let's say we have a company that has identified a perception (real or imagined) that supervisors are "playing favorites." If your employees are motivated by pragmatism or relevance, you might conduct small group meetings in order to identify which supervisors are biased or which policies are being administered unfairly. Armed with this information, you may either retrain supervisors, revise policies or educate employees about application of those policies (depending, of course, on whether the perception is real or imagined).

If fear is the prime motivator, however, the strategy changes. In this circumstance, small group sessions tend to be ineffective. Employees motivated by fear are unlikely to confide in managers or supervisors who may not act in the best interests of employees. Therefore, anonymous surveys (or focus groups conducted by outside consultants) become a valuable method for identifying supervisors or policies that may be problematic. These sessions should occur in the context of broader training in the areas of approachability and candor, and must be conducted with the participation of top management and line level supervisors. In this way trust can begin to develop among all levels of employees.

Depending on the history of the company, the process of identifying and managing these issues can take anywhere from a few months to several years. Moreover, certain issues may be "fear" issues while others may be "pragmatic" ones, requiring different approaches. The important thing is to identify the issues and develop a strategy around the motivation of employees instead of applying a "one-size fits all" solution to the problems of various groups of employees with a variety of motivations.

Moving From Fear to Relevance

As one may have surmised by now, the key to our strategy is to work toward moving the primary motivation behind issues from fear to relevance. As described earlier, this process is a continuum, and certain issues may always have fear as the underlying motivation. The key is to move as many issues as possible from fear to pragmatism and then from pragmatism to relevance. This means there is an educational process that must take place when solving any issue.

Implementing this educational process with employees first involves understanding and believing that the employer does have their best interests at heart. While they will not always agree with the employer, employees must not be allowed to believe that the employer does not care about their concerns. The next step is to educate employees about how and why decisions are made. This is a dialogue, and employees are given the opportunity to contribute ideas and provide input as to the successful operation of the company.

During this phase, employees can learn firsthand the pros and cons of various strategies. Employees are then more likely to make the pragmatic decision of sticking with their employer rather than turning to any outside third party. Finally, after establishing a history of solving problems together (particularly when the employer is perceived to value and actively collaborate with employees) the pragmatic motivation turns into one of relevance.

Client Story: Strategy Driven By Employee Motivation

One of the first things I try to assess with a new client is where he or she stands on the fear-pragmatism-relevance continuum. Recently we began working with a manufacturer who had four plants – one in the Southwest, one in the West, one in the Southeast and a new one in the Midwest. We conducted surveys at each location.

Interestingly, the four plants each had distinct personalities. The manufacturer's Southwest location was organized by the steelworkers and the working relationships there were quite hostile. This plant was a workplace primarily motivated by fear. The Midwest plant and the plant in the West were both "middle of the pack" with a good amount of uncertainty about job security issues. The plant in the Southeast was one of the highest rated organizations we have surveyed to date.

Our first order of business is always to communicate the results of the opinion surveys. We develop actions based on each company's "personality." As a result, we decided it was best to have our organization communicate the results of the survey to employees at the Southwest plant. These employees exhibited extreme distrust of management, according to the survey results. We determined that taking public action and communicating the results in focus group sessions with outside professionals would demonstrate the company's commitment to this plant. These sessions were sometimes heated, but each group expressed surprise that management actually invested time and effort to communicate the results. Some employees even said they would have answered a few of the questions differently if they believed management intended to seriously consider the results. As we explored each issue in depth, it turned out that much of the conflict was based on misperceptions – few employees could come up with concrete examples to back up poor scoring on certain statements. These sessions, while not an ultimate solution, provided an effective starting point for building bridges between management and its unionized employees.

The Western and Midwest plants required a different approach. While there was not open hostility toward management, these employees still faced significant issues that needed to be discussed. They also expressed concern about the direction local management was taking. We dispatched a corporate human resources representative to present the results at these locations.

We put together a communication package that the corporate human resources representative used to discuss the results and identify issues that the company would focus on in the coming months. To contend with these issues, specific action plans were outlined and teams created to respond to the issues raised. Local management at each plant was given

the key role of ensuring that these teams were given the opportunity to succeed. The process implemented in these plants constituted a more pragmatic approach.

The Southeast location had few issues and required little process implementation. Local management was dispatched to communicate the survey results and the areas where improvement should be made. While these meetings were (predictably) very positive, we instructed local management to make clear that the company was not content to rest on these accomplishments but would take action to improve in every area it could.

Many businesses rely on fear as a primary union-free motivation. Depending on the type of industry and its geographic location, this strategy may be sustainable for a few companies. However, this strategy is without a doubt the least sustainable and also the least productive in the long term. Relying on an employment environment driven by fear is precarious. Given the wrong set of circumstances, these companies can quickly become targets of unions and often are organized.

More important, in today's labor market these companies are not employers of choice – companies that rule by fear are more likely to have a high rate of employee turnover and will be less competitive, all things being equal, than competitors who stress an open and collaborative work environment. Employee relations is an area where the right thing to do is also the smart thing to do from a business perspective.

Employees motivated to remain union-free by pragmatism are a step further in the right direction. These employees have decided, perhaps through enlightened self-interest, that they do not want a union. The disadvantage of relying on this motivation is that it can be turned against a company – the SEIU is experiencing significant improvement in organizing health care units relying on this strategy. Although much preferable to fear, pragmatism is not a panacea.

In order to guarantee union-free status, a company must strive to make unions irrelevant to their employees. Creating a work environment where unions are seen as irrelevant is hard work. It is not enough to simply explain the disadvantages of unions. Employees must feel in their core that their company is a great place to work. The thought of unionization never crosses these employees' minds. If forced to confront the idea, the notion is comical to them. An employer who accomplishes this difficult task creates an employee relations environment that is collaborative, productive and generally more profitable.

Chapter 4

Third-Party Intervention, Vulnerability and Your Union- Free Strategy

"The art of being wise is the art of knowing what to overlook."
William James

What You'll Learn In This Chapter
- ❑ What is tpIQ and how do I figure it for my organization?
- ❑ How do I figure my organization's Employment Misery Index?
- ❑ How do I determine my organization's Regulatory Compliance Factor?
- ❑ What items should be part of a successful employment practices audit?
- ❑ How do I establish the Union Activity Profile for my area?
- ❑ What impact does my company's size have on my vulnerability?

Denial of the problem is the biggest obstacle in dealing with a company that has labor issues. Most employers believe they treat their employees right and feel very offended when their efforts at "good employee relations" are questioned.

Nothing is more depressing than seeing the president or owner of a business receive an NLRB petition for the first time. Their initial reaction is often one of shock. They find it difficult to believe that employees whom they consider family would betray them and their business. These employers are usually at a loss to explain what issues, if any, exist in their work force. When they begin to look, they find that the process of identifying the origins of the organizing campaign is both difficult and revealing.

Ultimately, employers faced with petitions learn that they ignored telltale signs of discontent among employees. This learning curve is steep and the process is an extremely expensive one. There are many costs associated with fighting an NLRB organizing campaign. These are often coupled with demoralizing battles against regulatory agencies and the court system. Further, the constraints of this legal environment often prevent employers from acting on their first impulse – fixing the problem.

Instituting proactive measures to improve the employment environment is the natural reaction of most employers, once they are notified of employee discontent. However, positive changes in terms or conditions of employment are many times considered bribes and ruled illegal. Likewise, team-based responses to employment issues are regularly disallowed in this environment. In sum, the employer's hands are tied.

Employers embroiled in this mess typically wish for one thing: that they had known of their employees' unhappiness prior to their turning to the union. Unfortunately, a symptom prevalent in these companies is that employees feel constrained in some way from discussing these problems with management, or worse, they have expressed their problems and been ignored.

I assist employers in turning back the clock. I give them the knowledge they would have after a union campaign, but in a pre-petition environment. I sum up these efforts in a concept called "tpIQ." TpIQ stands for "third party intervention quotient" and is a summary of a number of factors that identify vulnerability to outside intervention whether it be unions, government agencies or courts. The tpIQ concept is helpful in identifying vulnerability, but it is not a panacea.

No system exists that can tell you with complete accuracy whether your company will be attacked by a union or any other outside party. Human beings do not act as rationally as management consultants or company owners often would wish. At any time, and under a variety of almost infinite circumstances, employees can turn to outside third parties who are waiting and watching for the opportunity to intervene. The idea behind tpIQ is to help identify whether or not an outside third party would find "fertile ground" for intervention at a particular company. We believe the principles of the tpIQ concept embody many of the predictors of vulnerability to outsider intervention.

How Was tpIQ Developed?
The concepts of tpIQ have been developed over many years of work and practical application. Some are scientific while others are not. The program, like any work force, relies on several variables in determining vulnerability. As a means of isolating and managing these variables, surveys of almost a million employees in all major industry groupings have been conducted.

Employment Misery Index
The first area tested combines a number of factors that we call an employment misery index. Like the misery index for inflation, the employment misery index provides a gauge of how the employment environment in one company compares to the environments of companies benchmarked as being low-risk for outside intervention.

Another statistic very useful to know is how a particular company's misery index compares to that same company's index in earlier periods. Comparison of a company's index score to the overall scores of other companies in similar industries and geographic regions is another key piece of information provided by the data.

The employment misery index is not as broad-based as a typical employee opinion survey. Instead, the misery index concentrates on issues that tend to be flashpoints for outside intervention. The table below lists a number of the statement areas we survey to determine an accurate employment misery index.

For a person with my abilities, there are many opportunities for advancement.
I believe management and my immediate supervisor have a sincere interest in the people who work here.
The best way to get a raise here is to do a good job.
Around here, "what" you know is more important than "who" you know.
The channels of communication between employees and management are working satisfactorily.
I believe the benefits offered here are fair and reasonable when compared to similar employers in this area.
No one here is ever discriminated against.
I believe that pay increases are based on performance.
I am not aware of any instances of sexual harassment.
The way raises are determined here is fair.
People here get terminated only for good reasons.
My immediate supervisor is fair and consistent in the treatment of employees.
The most capable employees are always the ones selected for promotions.
My work area is safe and accidents are infrequent.
I believe management knows what employees think about most major

issues.
Considering the type of work I do, I feel my pay is fair for this area.
Our rules and regulations are uniformly administered.
Promotions are always based on performance.
I am treated fairly and with respect by my immediate supervisor.
My immediate supervisor judges me based on facts, rather than opinions, rumors and personality judgments.

The Regulatory Compliance Factor

The second major area we test to predict vulnerability is the regulatory compliance factor. This factor is determined by conducting a thorough labor and employment law audit of the target company. The theory behind the regulatory compliance factor is that the more a company complies with labor and employment law standards, the less likely it is to be vulnerable to intervention from government agencies and employment lawsuits. Regulatory non-compliance issues can also be a catalyst to union organizing campaigns.

A variety of different issues are analyzed when determining a company's regulatory compliance. Given the increasing number of statutes and regulations applied to and their workforces in the United States, a significant number of issues are examined in the regulatory compliance aspect of our review. A few of these are:

Employee Handbook	ADA Compliance
Sexual Harassment Policy	Family Medical Leave Act
Safety Programs	Overtime Compliance/Exempt Status
Hiring Practices	Independent Contractor Designation
Employment Testing	Dispute Resolution Programs

There are a number of other laws and regulations that employees can rely on for third party intervention. This list is not meant to be exhaustive, but does include some of the more likely areas where third party intervention often occurs. The table below lists a number of the issues we consider when assigning a regulatory compliance factor score to a client.

EMPLOYMENT AUDIT
My firm has audited its employment policies with the assistance of labor counsel in the last 12 months.
HANDBOOK - POLICIES
We have an employee handbook.
The employee handbook is distributed to all employees.
The employee handbook contains an acknowledgement form that is signed by the employee.
The employee handbook contains a valid "at-will" disclaimer at the beginning and on the signature page.
The employee handbook contains summaries of sexual harassment/discrimination, injury reporting requirements, FMLA, no solicitation, statement on unions, and progressive discipline.
The policies in the employee handbook are consistently applied by all managers/supervisors.
SEXUAL HARASSMENT - DISCRIMINATION
Our firm has a sexual harassment and nondiscrimination policy.
Our policy is posted.
Our policy is well communicated - employees and supervisors receive regular training on the policy and the complaint procedure, and this training is documented.
Our firm has an effective reporting and investigation procedure (including multiple routes for complaint/investigation).
FLSA - WAGE AND HOUR
Our firm has a clearly defined method of designating exempt and non-exempt employees.
Our exempt employees are paid on a salary basis for all hours worked.
Our non-exempt employees receive overtime for all hours worked over 40 in a week.
We have reviewed our state laws regarding wage payment, lunch and break periods, accrual of vacation pay and pay on termination and our policies are consistent with those regulations.
OSHA
Our firm has a well-designed safety program, including lockout/tagout, hazard communication and MSDS materials.
Our firm conducts regular training on safety issues as part of our safety program and this training is documented.
We have an effective reporting procedure for injuries.
WORKERS COMPENSATION, ADA, FMLA
Our firm has a consistent return-to-work policy for employees who are away from work due to injury or illness, whether work related or

not.
Our firm has a policy for determining when light duty or other accommodations should be made for injured or ill employees.
NLRA
Our supervisors are trained to recognize the early warning signs of union organizing as well as their rights and obligations under the NLRA.
Our firm has a valid, consistently enforced, no solicitation policy.

Reviewing these areas and ascertaining your firm's compliance will significantly reduce the likelihood of facing regulatory action or lawsuits based on unlawful employment practices.

Union Activity Profile

The third important factor we examine in determining a company's tpIQ is the union activity profile for the region in which your company is located. This factor looks at the organizing activity and examines contracts in effect in the immediate vicinity of a company. Finally, this part of the survey analyzes whether competitors or companies in and around the immediate vicinity of the surveyed location are unionized.

The intent of this factor is to identify areas where unions have already organized and determine if the activity is geographically based or industry based. This information allows us to surmise the risk factors for an individual business. By looking at union activity this way, we can more accurately predict the likelihood that an otherwise vulnerable company will become a target.

Obviously, there are a number of companies with poor employment misery index scores and low regulatory compliance factors that are never approached by unions. This often is due to the fact that unions are inactive in their region, or there are no unions proximately located that could economically organize the group of employees. The union activity profile helps to identify whether poor scores in other areas are likely to result in intervention by a union. The following table lists some of the factors we use when analyzing the union activity profile for clients.

Union Activity Profile
There have been few union petitions filed in my city, state and/or region in the last 18-24 months.
I am not aware of any card-signing activity in my community.
My employees do not have regular interaction with unionized employees of other companies.
My organization is not a highly visible non-union company in either a highly unionized sector or in a sector that has been designated a target area for unions recently.
None of my competitors are unionized.
The active unions in my area do not typically represent companies in my industry.
None of the companies in my physical vicinity are unionized or are threatened by organizing activity.

Many company executives are unaware of the resources available today to track union activity. For example, Labor Relations Institute tracks all petition activity, strike activity, election results and news articles on every union in the United States. This information is available online at www.lrionline.com. This information can also be tracked by periodically visiting your local regional office of the NLRB (or requesting, under the Freedom of Information Act, that the information to be sent to you). Reviewing local publications from unions is another great source of information, although getting on the mailing list can be tricky sometimes.

It is vital to remember that this factor deals exclusively with union intervention. Government intervention or intervention by plaintiffs' attorneys is certainly not precluded just because a company has a low union activity profile. In fact, these types of intervention are probably more likely in companies with a high employment misery index or low regulatory compliance factor but a low union activity profile, since employees will have limited options to complain about problems at work.

Company Size

This factor looks only at the number of employees concentrated in a company. From a unionization standpoint, larger groups of employees are more attractive targets because they represent greater potential income from union dues. Unions are more likely to expend great resources on units of over 100 employees than on very small units.

At the same time, there are often diminishing returns in attempting to organize an employer with thousands of employees, due to the huge investment of resources required to accomplish this goal. Larger employers are often much more sophisticated and capable of spending great amounts of resources to fight an organizing campaign. In addition, a limited number of targets (in 1999 there were under 10,000 employers with between 1,000 and 5,000 employees – many of whom are already organized) are at the very large end of the spectrum.

This does not mean small employers have nothing to fear. Many companies are not aware of the fact that union win rates also improve in smaller companies. In fact, many companies are surprised to know that the median election size has for many years been well under 30 employees. The median unit size in the latest data available (2002 petitions) is 25 employees. There is also an enormous number of targets (over 8 million in 1999) in the 1-9 employee range.

In order to develop the risk factor for employer size, we analyzed average petition activity over a three-year period and annualized it. This data, broken down by employer size, was then compared to a database of companies doing business in the United States. Based on these two data sets, a probability was assigned.

Based on this data, employer size – if very small or very large– tends to predict a lower likelihood of intervention by unions. Employer sizes in the mid- to large range (especially employers with between 100 and 1,000 employees) have a greater risk of union intervention. The table below describes generally how employer size relates to the probability of being petitioned for representation:

Employee Range	Union Vulnerability
1-9	1:10,000
10-19	1:1000
20-49	2:1000
50-99	3:1000
100-249	4:1000
250-499	6:1000
500-999	5:1000
1000-4999	2:1000

With respect to government intervention or intervention from plaintiffs' attorneys, the numbers work basically as one would predict: the larger the employer, the greater the likelihood of intervention by government agencies or lawsuits from plaintiffs' attorneys. Very small employers are often not covered by employment legislation at all, and this reduces the likelihood of being sued under one of these statutes. (State laws differ dramatically in these areas, so it is important to review both state and federal requirements.) In addition, the fewer employees, the fewer opportunities to be sued.

The following table summarizes a few of the major employment statutes and coverage requirements. You should consult the coverage of all laws (not just those listed here), both federal and state, for all locations in which you have employees.

Law	Who is covered?	Summary
Civil Rights Act of 1964 (Title VII)	Employers with 15 or more employees	Bars employment discrimination based on race, color, religion, sex, pregnancy or national origin
Americans with Disabilities Act	Employers with 15 or more employees	Bars discrimination against individuals with disabilities and requires public areas to be usable and accessible to disabled persons
Age Discrim. in Employment Act	Employers with 20 or more employees	Bars discrimination against persons aged 40 or older
Fair Labor Standards Act	All employers	Establishes minimum wage, overtime and child labor laws
Family and Medical Leave Act	Employers with 50 or more employees	Requires unpaid, job-protected leave up to 12 weeks per year
Occupational Safety and Health Act	All employers	Requires safety and health standards to avoid illness, harm or death
National Labor Relations Act	Employers meeting certain "interstate commerce" - covers most employers	Governs union organizing and collective bargaining

There are, of course, many other statutes, standards and theories under which an employer can be sued. This list only covers a few of the "highlights" that are often the most common sources of employee litigation. It is critical to regularly conduct audits of your company to identify potential liabilities under these or other statutes.

If you have any questions about the requirements of the laws in your state, or how to comply with the listed federal laws, it is important to discuss these with your labor counsel <u>before</u> you have a problem. Once you receive notification of a complaint, it is too late.

How Do I Use the tpIQ Score?

As mentioned earlier, the tpIQ score is an approximation of risk used to assess vulnerability. It is not an absolute indication and there are certainly companies that might score well on the factors described and still be subject to an organizing attempt or government intervention. By the same token, the worse a company performs on these factors, the greater the likelihood that some type of intervention will occur in that company.

We use the tpIQ score as a departure point for determining what priorities should be developed in a particular organization. For example, if the regulatory compliance score is high but the employment misery index is low, we would recommend that a company concentrate more on employee relations efforts, possibly beginning with a comprehensive employee opinion survey on all employment issues. Conversely, a company with a high employment misery index score and a low regulatory compliance score is more likely in need of a comprehensive employment audit. In cases where both scores are in the high range, comprehensive efforts are probably unnecessary.

Employee Opinion Surveys - Your Employees Know Whether They Want a Union – Ask Them!

"Where an opinion is general, it is usually correct."
Jane Austen, Mansfield Park

What You'll Learn In This Chapter
- ❑ Why conducting an opinion survey on the heels of a union election is a good strategy
- ❑ The types of opinion surveys you should consider
- ❑ What you should know about "whole system" or appreciative inquiry methods
- ❑ Key considerations when constructing your survey
- ❑ How to tabulate your survey information
- ❑ The best ways to communicate survey results to your employees
- ❑ Legal issues regarding the conduct of opinion surveys in a "post-campaign" environment

The first step to designing your strategy is discovery – identify the issues that you need to respond to. As discussed earlier, the method you use in discovery will depend on the primary motivation of your workforce. I have found that in most post-campaign organizations (but certainly not all of them – more on that later) an anonymous, forced-response survey is an effective method of discovery.

There are three important reasons we often start with an opinion survey. Surveys provide a road map for problem solving, facilitate communication in companies that do not communicate well and provide a baseline from which a company can benchmark progress.

Effectively administered surveys provide critical information about the primary problem areas and map out the most logical path to solutions. Surveys identify problem areas particular to specific groups and those common to the company. This information provides a road map and priority list for dealing with problems in all areas. The order in which problems are dealt with is not always dictated by the ones employees feel worst about. Nevertheless, ranking the issues first puts some logic into the system of designing a plan for attacking employee relations problems.

It is also critical, particularly in companies that have undergone union organizing attempts, to initiate communication by asking for employee input and appropriately responding to that input when it is received. The most effective method for gleaning opinions from employees and formulating a response is a formal survey. By conducting an employee opinion survey and communicating the results of the survey, a company is well positioned to formalize a communication process in its workforce.

Finally, the survey results provide a snapshot of employee attitude at a moment in the life of your company. Starting from this point you can later identify, in an objective and scientific way, whether the company is making progress or backsliding. While administering a survey is not the only method of providing this benchmark, the information gained provides a background with which to interpret other necessary data such as turnover statistics and numbers of grievances or complaints filed by employees. Survey information is a critical piece of the puzzle and, if used properly, can pinpoint areas for improvement.

Surveys on the Heels of Union Elections

Companies we have assisted through union elections are often reluctant to conduct opinion surveys. "Look, our employees already think we stink," they might say "We've been hearing it for over a month now. Why don't we just let this thing die down for a month or two – Lord knows we could focus a little more on our core business around here." These companies suffer from campaign myopia. In our experience, this is the perfect time to conduct the survey.

It is true that employees who have recently been through a campaign are normally more negative about management, particularly top management. The union has spent several weeks, if not months, questioning every move made and characterizing all company moves as evil and motivated by greed. Companies that have suffered through this process, even if they ultimately prevail, are wary of giving employees another opportunity to take a shot at them. This view is short sighted and leads more often than not to another petition a year later.

These companies fail to appreciate context. Companies attacked by unions typically have a poor history of communicating with their employees. During the weeks preceding the union election, many managers and supervisors spend more time talking to employees than they ever have before. This often becomes a reason that many "fence-sitters" vote for the company in the election – they have a new relationship with their supervisor or manager and they believe things will change after the election.

Companies often believe that this will happen too, as a natural side effect of the campaign. It often never does. The sad fact is that managers and supervisors often (and usually unintentionally) slip into the bad habits of the past.

In addition, there is a group of employees (sometimes almost half of the workforce) who wanted to have a union and are looking for management to return to its old ways. These employees, often prompted by the union organizers who helped them during the campaign, will continue to look for reasons to attack management. They'll be saying things like, "See, what did we tell you – business as usual. Well, you guys really screwed things up for us this year, but just wait until next time – we'll get that union in here then!"

In many ways, this negativity becomes a self-fulfilling prophesy. Even the employees who want to believe management will learn its lesson from the campaign need evidence. Otherwise, they will begin to believe that minority of the workforce that wants management to fail.

Employers must act quickly after the election to give their employees reason to believe things will be different. By taking a formal and public action on the heels of the campaign, management gives its supporters evidence that things will be different. The "fence-sitters" will give the company some time. The negative employees will, of course, begin knocking the company at every opportunity, but their audience will be limited at first.

Clearly things will be negative on this survey – employees do not invite unions into workplaces that have no problems. Nevertheless, the company has to start somewhere. Using this admitted "low point" in

the company's history acts both as motivation to improve and helps ensure that there is significant room to improve. By completing the survey and quickly communicating the results, management takes leadership on the communication issue.

This is not to say that the survey is a "ploy" or is just a way for the company to buy time. Any company using the survey in this way is kidding itself – failure to attack the issues that led to an organizing campaign will lead to another and, ultimately, a bargaining obligation. But acting quickly and publicly gives the company an opportunity to make significant progress on the issues that matter most to its employees.

Employee opinion surveys are not a panacea. They can be very problematic, which explains why some employers are reluctant to use them. There are a number of potential pitfalls to opinion surveys. Often employers are appalled at their results and hesitate to reveal them. However, companies must commit to communicating the results – good, bad or otherwise. We tell our clients to forget about a survey unless they are committed to communicating the results honestly. In fact, conducting an employee opinion survey without this commitment is worse than not conducting a survey at all.

Therefore, it is important to know ahead of time how you plan to communicate both the delivery of the survey and the results once the data is collected. Additionally, since employee opinion surveys can take many different forms, it is important to pick a format that has the highest likelihood of success in the unit you are surveying. The following information describes various survey formats and their respective strengths and weaknesses.

Anonymous Forced Response.

This is a survey format that our firm commonly uses in units that have recently suffered a union campaign. The anonymous forced response survey is usually a form containing various statements regarding work environment. Respondents are forced to mark their degree of agreement or disagreement with the statements.

One advantage of this type of survey is its anonymity. The survey can be administered in such a way that members of management are precluded from seeing the actual survey questionnaires filled out by employees. This promise of anonymity helps some employees overcome the fear of negative job implications for answering questions honestly. As a result, most employees feel that they can be more candid in this type of survey.

It is important to note that even this type of survey can have skewed results. For example, in a unit where a group of employees conspire to answer all questions negatively or positively, the results obviously will be inaccurate. This problem is not unique to the anonymous forced response survey, but it can more difficult to detect.

The primary disadvantage of the anonymous forced response survey is that the information gathered is limited by the specificity of the questions asked. If the questions are not framed properly, employees may not be able to communicate all the problems or concerns they face. In addition, several different questions must be asked concerning the same issue. Otherwise there is a risk that the wording of a single question might skew responses toward the positive or negative.

Open-ended questions are good to add to forced response surveys. This provides a method to voice issues not covered in the forced response section, or for clarification of answers to that section. While some employees may not respond to the open-ended questions (fearful that management might see the surveys) it provides a good way to correct for any problems in crafting the forced-response questions. Concerns about anonymity can also be handled during the administration of the survey.

Finally, there are a number of administration issues that can skew survey results. For example, where management retaliation is an issue, less candid results are obtained if a management employee administers or gathers the completed surveys. Another important factor is to administer the survey to groups of employees in as similar circumstances as possible. For example, large time gaps between survey administration periods can alter results markedly. We recommend that companies conduct surveys in small blocks of time, no longer than a week.

Large Group or "Whole-System" Meetings

A less often used, but also highly effective method of discovery is the whole-system meeting. These meetings, used most often in strategy or planning contexts, invite as many employees as possible (often the entire organization – hence the name whole-system change) into a large meeting room. These meetings are based on the "systems" philosophy of organizations that holds that any change to a system must engage that entire system to be effective. These meetings can be very powerful and, if done well, can result in immediate and long-lasting change in an organization.

The advantage of whole-system meetings is that they do engage the entire system. Usually mixed groups of employees and managers sit together and discuss a number of questions regarding where the company has been and where it is going, The groups are asked to report back to the whole system and key ideas are recorded. Often groups are asked to record their thoughts in pictures or on video. These meetings are very effective when conducted from an appreciative inquiry perspective (for more on appreciative inquiry, see the sidebar *Appreciative Inquiry* in this chapter).

There are two key disadvantages to whole-system methods. First, the meetings are open and are intended to go wherever the system wants; in fact strict management control signals that the company is not interested in employee opinion. Lack of control is unsettling for management groups that are not used to employee involvement. In addition, the meetings can get out of control or become negative, particularly in a post-campaign environment. For this reason it is best that professionals experienced in facilitating whole-system meetings be in charge of the early meetings.

One-on-One or Small Group Interviews
This method of surveying overcomes many of the disadvantages of the forced response survey method. In this type of survey, a management representative or outside consultant conducts individual or small group interview sessions with a representative sample of employees.

These interviews typically follow a consistent format. Employees are asked to comment on various issues and discussion then ensues regarding reactions to the various issues discussed. Notes of the meeting are kept, and a record of the various responses to questions and issues is made, which summarizes the comments of the various groups surveyed.

The primary advantage of the focus group opinion survey is its free style. Employees are encouraged to talk about any or all issues affecting them. Employee input typically feeds on itself and often a variety of pertinent issues are raised in these discussions. Due to the need for a representative sampling of employees, employees should get opinions from all areas of the company.

In conducting these sessions, employers will also receive opinions and input about many different aspects of the operation. A major advantage of the focus group method over a forced response survey is that if the forced response survey fails to ask a question about an important area, input on that issue may never come up during that survey. Those topics will definitely come up during a focus group session.

However, there are disadvantages to the focus group method. A primary obstacle is finding an able leader of the focus groups. A critical factor for success is to have a facilitator who can manage focus group sessions in a positive and productive way. Often these meetings raise contentious issues and can become highly charged and negative. This is not always a disadvantage, but employees must feel free to comment on issues.

A leader must be able to keep sessions productive and deter personal attacks. The leader should be a capable facilitator who is interested in gaining insight into all sides of an issue. Obviously a meeting facilitated by a manager who is dominant or viewed negatively is not conducive to an open meeting format.

Another disadvantage of these meetings is they can be dominated by a few people or select issues. These events can skew survey results. An unskilled facilitator may allow only a few individuals to dominate the discussion. This can markedly limit viewpoints and perspectives. This is the "squeaky wheel" problem with focus group surveys. In the same way, a particularly public or heated problem can dominate discussion and remove focus completely from other issues that are just as important.

A good facilitator can resolve these concerns in some respects, but they are inherent weaknesses in the focus group system. If employees are fired up about an issue, this opportunity will allow that issue to dominate their discussion. This situation makes it very difficult to get much discussion about other issues that, while they may be problems, are not as important at the time of the survey. A final disadvantage of the focus group method is that it is not anonymous. Depending on the identity of the facilitator, employees may be very hesitant to openly discuss sensitive management issues.

One-on-one interviews can also be effective methods of discerning employees opinion. These interviews can be used not only to learn employee opinion, but also to increase faith in a particular leader. I have had clients use a simple model developed by a navy ship captain named Mike Abrashoff[5]. He used a simple three-question survey of his entire crew when he took over the USS *Benfold*. Those questions were: What do you like most about the *Benfold*? What do you like least? What would you change if you could?

---

[5] *See* Polly Labarre, "Grassroots Leadership: USS *Benfold*," 23 Fast Company 115-126 (1999); and Michael Abrashoff, *It's Your Ship: Management Techniques from the Best Damn Ship in the Navy* (Warner Books, 2002).

One-on-one interviews can have some of the same problems as small group sessions. Depending on the ability of the person conducting the interviews, employees may not feel comfortable opening up. These meetings can be intimidating for some employees. This can raise potential legal concerns.[6]

Once again, these issues may be resolved with a skilled facilitator. In our experience if a company leader really takes these meetings seriously they can have tremendous impact on both morale and the organization's effectiveness. However, a leader that looks at the meetings as a "chore" will fail to accomplish anything by going through the motions.

Supervisory Focus Groups

This method of survey is one level removed from surveying the opinions of line-level employees. In this method, focus group meetings are held with line-level supervisors and department managers. These meetings are typically conducted much like those for hourly employee focus groups. A facilitator, either a high-level company manager or an outside consultant, will ask a series of questions about the company and try to get the pulse of overall employee opinion based on the opinions of supervisors who work most closely with the hourly employees.

The big advantage to this method is that it is the least disruptive to the work of hourly employees. Also, this process requires less time and reduces interruption of company operations. Another advantage is that this method can prevent built-up expectations in the workforce. For instance, often hourly employees believe that, after vocalizing their complaints,

---

[6] *See infra.* at 74.

management will immediately act. Since hourly employees are not directly asked about complaints under this method, there is less likelihood that employees will blame management for not immediately solving issues vocalized in the meetings.

However, supervisory focus group processing is less effective in some respects. The method relies heavily on the capability of line-level supervisors, who are often the weak link in companies susceptible to third party intervention. It is, however, a method of getting a quick "lay of the land" in determining which of the other two strategies is best suited for the company.

Other Methods of Ascertaining Employee Opinion

Many other methods can be used by employers to learn employee opinion. Open door policies, suggestion procedures, one-on-one conversations and the like are a few. We do not characterize these methods as effective ways of driving and evaluating company-wide opinion. While these means can certainly be important aspects to any employee relations program, exclusive use of these methods will not effectively deliver the information a company needs to design a third-party intervention strategy. The chapter on employee communications programs describes some effective strategies and means of implementation to get these programs working in your company.

Tabulating Opinion Survey Results

One of the most important aspects of conducting an employee opinion survey is tabulating the results appropriately. A scientific, statistical approach must be used to tabulate this information in order to achieve optimal results. Collecting groups of random comments without proper categorizing is a sure recipe for disorganization and, ultimately, failure. Issues must be coordinated among logical employee work groups in order to clearly plan how to attack problems that are identified (and even which problems to attack). No matter which method of gathering opinion is utilized, it is necessary to organize the data in a way that is useful for strategy and planning purposes.

The first principle of organizing opinion survey data is to group comments into categories of opinion. For example, comments regarding pay and benefits should be separated from comments regarding policies, procedures and other matters. The table below lists the categories of behavior LRI Management Services assesses during employee opinion surveys. Of course, categories can be added or subtracted based on the specific needs and issues of the company.

Work Conditions	Training
Job Satisfaction	Immediate Supervisor
Company Pride	Communications
Pay and Benefits	Work Relations
Advancement	Top Management

In addition to categorizing opinion according to question category, the results are also tabulated according to other applicable categories, i.e.:

Department	Sex
Shift	Race
Supervisor	Plant Location
Job Classification	Product Line

By breaking survey results down according to these areas, we can pinpoint exactly where problems are occurring in the workforce and where they are not.

Failure to break results down into work group categories like these can often hide significant problems in the company. Some groups may be more positive and mask the scores of groups that are more negative. Pivoting the data in these various ways provides the clearest picture of the company and creates opportunities to attack issues that may have remained hidden under other methods.

Constructing Your Survey

We typically ask seven statements in each category in a "Likert-type" scale (each statement is ranked from 1 to 7, 1 being most disagreement and 7 being most agreement).[7] In this way we avoid the wording of one statement skewing the survey results. The scores on these seven statements are then combined to get the category score. At the conclusion of this book (*See* Appendix 1) is a sample basic survey, to give an idea of format.

Statement wording should be carefully considered. Statements should not be vague or subject to varied interpretations. They should cover observable behavior as opposed to thoughts or motives.[8] Since the Likert-type scale is designed to capture degree of agreement or disagreement, it is better to word questions directly and mildly positive or negative ("My immediate supervisor treats workers consistently" is better than "Managers usually treat workers well").

---

[7] There is some debate in the academic literature regarding the validity of using various numbers of response categories in a Likert-type scale (i.e. 5, 7, 9 or more responses). *Cf.* PAUL KLINE, HANDBOOK OF PSYCHOLOGICAL TESTING 189 (2d ed. 2000) (7-point scale is most reliable) *with* LEWIS R. AIKEN, RATING SCALES & CHECKLISTS 238 (1996) (5- point scale best, although 7-point scale may be best where range of attitudes are small). We prefer the 7-item scale for employee attitude measurement.

[8] *See* Palmer Morrel-Samuels, "Getting the Truth Into Workplace Surveys," Harvard Business Review 111-118 (February 2002).

Survey designers can add even more reliability into the instrument by some of the statements in the positive and some in the negative (*i.e.* "My immediate supervisor treats workers consistently" and "My immediate supervisor does not treat workers consistently"), preventing someone from skewing results by marking the same answer on every statement.[9] It can also help to ask a few items that can be independently verified.[10]

Appreciative Inquiry[11]

As mentioned earlier, there are numerous other ways to engage in discovery in a system besides engaging in surveys asking critical questions of management. Some observers even argue that asking employees to think about or list the problems in an organization creates both the (often unrealistic) expectation that the problems will be solved and (more important) further ingrains the idea that the organization itself is a problem to be solved. These observers look at organization life as more organic and fluid and less systematic. One of the most exciting areas of study to come from this perspective is that of Appreciative Inquiry.

Appreciative Inquiry was developed by Dr. David Cooperridder of Case Western Reserve University. This view holds that organizations are organic and constantly changing, much like the humans that make up the organization. Drawing on diverse fields like Gestalt psychology and medicine (studies of the Pygmalion effect, the Placebo effect and the effects of

---

[9] *See* KLINE, *supra* note 7, at 188-190 (2000).

[10] *See* Morrel-Samuels, *supra* note 8.

[11] For a broad survey of current thinking on the issue of Appreciative Inquiry and its application to organization development, *see* DAVID L. COOPERRIDER, ET. AL. APPRECIATIVE INQUIRY: RETHINKING HUMAN ORGANIZATION TOWARD A POSITIVE THEORY OF CHANGE (2000).

positive and negative self-talk on patient recovery rates) these researchers have concluded that the historic engineering-driven approach to organization development is in many ways based on a flawed model.

These researchers believe that the "culture" of an organization is simply a shorthand way to represent the thousands of conversations that occur each day between each member of the organization. The "vision" of the organization is really a shorthand way to represent the combined imagined futures of each of the individuals in the organization.

From this perspective, asking employees to criticize or problem solve their organization is counterproductive. It does not focus attention on where there is life in the system, but instead on where the system is failing. Instead of focusing on strength and possibility, the engineering mindset focuses on weakness and hopelessness.

Appreciative Inquiry asks the members of the system to concentrate on possibility and the things that give life to the system. Since the belief is that the conversations between group members *are the culture*, in this way the system is immediately energized and changed. By inquiring about what group members appreciate about their organization, they are implicitly invited to both celebrate and imagine how these aspects of the system can be brought to bear on its current challenges. Often many "problems" are "solved" using this approach, without ever expressly seeking out the problems or the solutions.

Organizations like British Airways, Roadway Express, Verizon and Avon have successfully utilized the

Appreciative approach in their organization development initiatives. The approach has significant possibilities for organizations that have recently experienced the negativity of a union organizing campaign. We utilize the approach in designing survey questions as well as when conducting live on-site interventions with large groups, small groups and teams. I include an example of using Appreciative Inquiry to identify your key employee relations objectives in Chapter 15.

There can be problems with breaking down data too narrowly. If the size of the work unit is small, or if the number of breakdowns is too numerous, there is the real possibility that only a few employees will fit into any one category. This creates two major problems. First, it can reduce the reliability of data, due to the fact that employees may fear that management will be able to identify individual employees who made a comment. This may result in employees answering untruthfully to statements about their supervisor or management.

There are also legal issues raised by the National Labor Relations Board regarding surveys that identify the individual making comments. *See infra* at 77. Therefore, it is vital to reach a good balance between enough data to make strong recommendations and too much data, which can negatively impact the results of the survey.

Care should also be taken in determining how opinion is evaluated among the categories and work groupings because there are several different ways to look at issues. For example, one might look at the overall average score in a particular work grouping. Another angle is to compare the percentage of employees who responded favorably to those who responded unfavorably. The results can also reveal specific numbers of employees who have rated statements at various levels of agreement or disagreement along the spectrum. There are advantages and disadvantages to each type of rating, and all three should be used to best analyze issues in a company.

Overall Scores

Overall scores are good for gauging, in general terms, how a group feels about a particular statement or category. These overall scores are misleading at times because extremely high ratings can sometimes mask a significant negative opinion on a question or issue. For example, a department consisting of three shifts may have very strong favorable opinions on first and second shifts but extremely negative opinions on third shift. While a significant problem exists on the third shift, it is not evident in the overall score. As a result, a company may be unaware of a significant employee relations issue.

Percent Favorable to Percent Unfavorable

This method is effective for determining significant pockets of favorable or unfavorable opinion. It allows a company to pinpoint where extremes have pulled a score up or down. However, percent favorable to unfavorable does not give as accurate a view of the overall feeling of a work grouping as the overall average score. This is because the favorable and unfavorable ratings can be spread across various degrees of agreement or disagreement. For example, a company may have an evenly distributed number of favorable and unfavorable responses, as a percentage, but those responses may be unevenly distributed within the favorable and unfavorable categories. See Appendix 2 for an example. In other words, two companies with the same percent favorable to percent unfavorable groupings could have significantly different overall scores on the same issue.

Actual Response Distribution
The advantage of this method is that a picture is formed of how employees feel on particular issues across the entire spectrum of responses. This method takes out the "averaging effect" of using overall favorable to unfavorable responses. The possible disadvantage of this method is that it creates information overload in some respects. In other words, negative opinion is expressed to many questions. Without some sense of the overall score of a particular group, it becomes increasingly difficult to prioritize action areas.

Therefore, it is easy to see the importance of using all available information, broken down in a variety of ways, to determine exactly which areas deserve the most consideration in a particular company.

Communicating Survey Results
The most important part of the process of administering and tabulating an effective employee opinion survey is communicating the results. If a company fails to communicate its survey results effectively, the survey can do more harm than good. Again, there are a variety of methods for communicating survey results to a work group. A few of those strategies are discussed here.

Small Group Sessions
This is the most common method of communicating survey results. A variety of reasons make this method desirable. First the small group is more manageable in most companies. Between 10 and 20 employees in a group helps to prevent disruptions but is still a large

enough group that people do not feel like they are being singled out.

The small group sessions should be delivered in a consistent manner. We typically recommend for companies to have a formal 15-minute presentation regarding the employee opinion survey results and then about another 15-minute block of time for questions and answers. Depending on the results of the survey, more time may be necessary. A model for this meeting is outlined in the table below.

MEETING AGENDA
RECAP OF SURVEY DESIGN
PRESENT SURVEY RESULTS
COMPARISONS WITH LAST YEAR
CONCLUSIONS FROM SURVEY
ACTION PLAN

Individual Meetings or Small Groups

For some businesses, especially small companies or ones in which large numbers of employees are not available at any particular time, this is the only effective method of delivering survey results in a meeting environment. The advantage of an intimate group is that the communication sessions can be custom tailored for the audience.

The disadvantage to this method is that it takes a significantly larger commitment of time to deliver results in this fashion. Small group sessions can be intimidating for the employees involved. Some workers might feel uncomfortable sitting alone with their supervisor discussing survey results – they may even think the supervisor knows how they responded to the survey. This scenario also raises concerns under the National Labor Relation Act, as discussed below. This is not our recommended method of delivering survey results.

Handouts Without a Meeting
This method is better suited for very large companies or companies where employee meetings are virtually impossible. These companies will create a handout that describes many of the same things described during a communication meeting. The advantage of this method is that it ensures consistent communication across all groups of employees. The disadvantage is that it is impersonal and requires a significant amount of effort in crafting the document.

In addition, employers should be aware that such a document could be used as a tool during future organizing attempts or in litigation against the company. Complaints raised in the survey might be used to prove later that an employer failed to take action to mitigate, for example, discrimination complaints. Union supporters will use the negative scores as evidence the company should be organized. These are not, by the way, reasons to avoid communicating survey results – they instead are reasons to take extra care in communicating the results and reacting to complaints raised.

Large Group Meetings
The large group meeting format is often the only method available for some companies. The sessions are very similar to the small group sessions outlined above. The disadvantage of large group meetings is that they can be unwieldy and hard to control. Some employees are intimidated when speaking in very large groups.

In addition, particularly for companies that have recently undergone organizing activities, the possibility exists that overly negative employees will showboat or take over the meeting. These problems can ruin an otherwise excellent opportunity to begin the healing process in a company. For these reasons, meetings should be facilitated by an experienced individual. If these situations are present, it is best to hold smaller group sessions where the overly negative individuals can be isolated in one group.

Use of Graphics
We highly recommend the use of some type of graphic presentation when communicating survey results. A variety of different representations of statistical information are available. There are also a variety of different ways to use the information. In the table shown in Appendix 2 you will see three examples of graphical representations of statistical information we gather on surveys. These demonstrate the three types of responses, overall scores, distribution between satisfaction and dissatisfaction, and distribution among each response.

While graphs and charts of this nature can be overused in a presentation, it is a good idea to use them at various times when particularly complicated ideas are being expressed. These graphics can be used in overhead slides, PowerPoint presentations and handouts to employees. Again, the key concept is to use the graphs and charts to supplement the information being communicated as opposed to relying on them to communicate the information.

Legal Issues
There are a number of legal considerations when planning an opinion survey. These fall into one of two categories. First, there are a number of National Labor Relations Board ("the Board" or "NLRB" hereafter) decisions regarding the use of opinion

surveys. The second area of concern is in responding to complaints of discrimination or safety violations that come up on the survey. Failure to respond to these issues can lead to potential liability under Title VII of the Civil Rights Act of 1964 or under the Occupational Safety and Health Act.

The NLRB has held in some circumstances that employee opinion surveys can violate the National Labor Relations Act ("the Act" or "NLRA" hereafter). These decisions center on the Board's interpretation of Section 8(a)(1) of the Act, which has been interpreted over the years as prohibiting the solicitation of grievances by management during union organizing activity.

Section 8(a)(1) of the NLRA provides that "it shall be an unfair labor practice for an employer to interfere with, restrain or coerce employees in the exercise of rights guaranteed in section 7." This section (as interpreted through Board decisions) prohibits employers from soliciting grievances where a purpose of such solicitation is to induce employees to reject a union as their collective bargaining agent. [12]

The Board will inquire into both the wording of the survey instrument as well as related comments made by representatives of management to determine whether either an express or implied promise of benefit is made to employees.[13] Perhaps the best expression of this doctrine was made in the Board's decision in *Uarco Incorporated*, 216 NLRB 1, 1-2 (1974) where it stated:

> . . . it is not the solicitation of grievances itself that is coercive and violative of Section 8(a)(1), but the promise to correct grievances or a

[12] See *Clark Equipment Company*, 278 NLRB 498, 516 (1986); *Ben Franklin Division of City Products Corporation*, 251 NLRB 1512, 1518 (1971).
[13] See *Clark Equipment*, 278 NLRB at 517.

concurrent interrogation or polling about union sympathies that is unlawful; the solicitation of grievances merely raises an inference that the employer is making such a promise, which inference is rebuttable by the employer.

Depending on the factual circumstances, the NLRB has held that some employee opinion surveys violate section 8(a)(1) as solicitations of grievances, while others do not. [14] The Board relies on a number of factors when determining whether a survey violates the prohibition on soliciting grievances, including the existence of union activity, the types of questions asked, whether participants are anonymous, whether the company has conducted surveys in the past, whether issues brought up in the survey are corrected and the timing of the survey.[15]

In *Clark Equipment Company* a union election was first held in February of 1978, in which the union lost.

---

[14] *Cf. Grove Valve and Regulator Company*, 262 NLRB 285 (1982) (opinion survey lawful where prior survey conducted in same unit absent union activity and questionnaire stated three times that survey does not imply changes in wages, benefits or work conditions) and *Leland Stanford Jr. University*, 240 NLRB 1138 (1978)(survey lawful where, although administered in pre-election context, no active campaigning occurred during the period before or after the survey and no election was scheduled or imminent) and *Clark Equipment*, 278 NLRB 498 (1986)(survey lawful where conducted 11 months after election and during time where there was no special union activity) with *Mid-State Distributing Company*, 276 NLRB 1511 (1985)(survey unlawful where no surveys were ever conducted prior to union organizing activity, and where employees were told during meetings that the problems that came up during the survey would be addressed by the company) and *Ben Franklin*, 251 NLRB 1512 (1971)(opinion survey unlawful where first formal survey conducted during midst of very active organizing campaign and where employer quickly made changes in wages, benefits and work conditions in response to survey) and *Tom Wood Pontiac, Inc.*, 179 NLRB 581 (1969), *enfd.* 447 F.2d 383 (7th Cir. 1971)(survey unlawful where conducted one week after stipulated election agreement and survey organizer repeatedly discussed correcting issues that came out of survey).

[15] See *e.g. Clark Equipment Company*, 278 NLRB 498, 516 (1986); *Ben Franklin*, 251 NLRB 1512, 1518 (1971).

The union objected to the first election and the NLRB, agreeing with the union objections, set aside the election and directed a second election. A second election was conducted in July of 1979, and the union lost again. Once again the union filed objections to the election. In May of 1980, while the NLRB considered the objections to the second election, the company announced and conducted a survey by distributing a questionnaire to all employees in its manufacturing operation.

The survey questionnaire was not the first survey conducted by the employer, who had earlier surveyed randomly selected groups of employees and on a separate occasion surveyed its supervisors. However, these earlier surveys were substantially different than the survey distributed in 1980.

The survey asked about policies and procedures, whether the company was a good place to work and whether employee complaints received attention. It also contained an open-ended question asking what employees would change about the company. The employer asserted that the survey was confidential, but employees were asked to reveal their department, work shift, sex and length of employment. The union filed an unfair labor practice charge alleging that the survey violated section 8(a)(1) of the Act.

The NLRB ruled that the survey did not violate the Act. The Board found that the survey, conducted 11 months after the second election and at a time when no "special union activity" was under way, did not unlawfully solicit grievances.[16] They ruled the survey lawful in spite of the conclusion that the survey could identify individual employee opinions on questions

---

[16] *Clark Equipment*, 278 NLRB at 517.

that could readily disclose employees' union sentiments.[17]

In *Ben Franklin,* the employer opened a distribution center in 1978 and union activity began almost immediately after the facility opened. In April of 1979, the union filed a petition to represent the employees of the facility, with an election scheduled for July 13. On June 6, the employer announced an employee opinion survey and asked employees to complete a survey form. One employee asked whether the surveys were being conducted because of the union activity and was told no and that surveys were common. The employer testified that, while informal surveys of a sampling of employees were common at other facilities, they decided to conduct a more formal survey using a questionnaire at this facility.

Follow-up meetings were conducted later in June, where the survey results were communicated to employees. The employer representative explained that the survey showed that communication between employees and supervisors needed improvement, and that there were questions about benefits and about wages. Employees were told during the meeting that the company would train the supervisors and that they would learn about wages in July. In early July the company announced pay increases to go into effect over the next year. Insurance plans were also explained.

The Board held that the conduct of the opinion survey violated section 8(a)(1) of the Act. Among the critical factors noted in the decision were that the survey did not follow the same pattern as other surveys, the survey occurred during the middle of a very active

---

[17] *Id.*

organizing effort and that the employer made improvements in wages and work conditions as a result of the survey.[18]

Holding individual or very small group meetings with employees can, under certain circumstances, also run afoul of the Act's protections. A number of Board decisions have found that, when an employee meeting occurs at a time, place or with personnel such that the employee may feel threatened or intimidated, the employer has engaged in unlawful interrogation under the Act.[19] The Board will examine all the surrounding circumstances when determining whether an employer's meeting was conducted in such a manner as to be threatening to the employee.[20]

In order to avoid problems with individual meetings, it is suggested that employer's begin these meetings by reassuring employees under the guidelines established in the Board's *Johnnie's Poultry* decision.[21] These safeguards were articulated in the context of questioning an employee regarding the investigation of an unfair labor practice charge. Nevertheless they are considered persuasive by the NLRB.[22]

The *Johnnie's Poultry* safeguards are as follows: (1) The purpose of the questioning must be

---

[18] *Ben Franklin*, 251 NLRB at 1519.

[19] *See e.g. Huntsville Mfg. Co.* 211 NLRB 54 (1974), *enforcement denied*, 514 F.2d 723 (5th Cir. 1972) (threat interfered election even though only one percent of employees threatened; enforcement denied due to union losing election by large majority); *Super Thrift Markets*, 233 NLRB 409 (1977).

[20] *See Blue Flash Express*, 109 NLRB 591 (1954).

[21] *Johnnie's Poultry Co.*, 146 NLRB 770 (1964), *enforcement denied*, 344 F.2d 617 (8th Cir. 1965) (denied on the basis that factual determinations not based on substantial evidence, did not express disagreement with the legal standards identified).

[22] The Board will quickly find an employer has violated 8(a)(1) if the safeguards are not followed in the context of questioning an employee regarding an unfair labor practice trial. *See e.g.* Kyle & Stephen, Inc. 259 NLRB 731 (1981).

communicated to the employee. (2) An assurance of no reprisal must be given. (3) The employee's participation must be obtained on a voluntary basis. (4) The questioning must take place in an atmosphere free from union animus. (5) The questioning itself must not be coercive in nature. (6) The questions must be relevant to the issues involved in the complaint. (7) The employee's subjective state of mind must not be probed. (8) The questions must not "otherwise interfere with the statutory rights of employees."[23] Explaining these issues to an employee prior to an individual meeting should provide a significant measure of protection to any potential unfair labor practice charge.

Another legal consideration regards complaints of discrimination. Employers have an obligation under Title VII of the Civil Rights Act of 1964 to avoid discrimination on the basis of race, color, religion, sex or national origin.[24] Other statutes prohibit discrimination based on age and disability.[25]

An employer who is made aware of discrimination or harassment based on a protected characteristic has an affirmative obligation to investigate and deal with those concerns.[26] Therefore, an employer who learns of discrimination based on a protected characteristic during an employee opinion survey must promptly conduct a thorough investigation of that claim and

---

[23] *Id.*

[24] 42 U.S.C. § 2000e *et seq.*

[25] See *e.g.* 42 U.S.C. §621 *et seq.* (Age Discrimination in Employment Act); 42 U.S.C. § 12101 *et seq.* (Americans With Disabilities Act of 1990).

[26] See *e.g. Burlington Industries v. Ellerth*, 524 U.S. 742 (1998)(one factor considered in employer affirmative defense to sex harassment cases is prompt investigation of claims); *Farragher v. City of Boca Raton*, 524 U.S. 775 (1998)(prompt investigation of claims is one factor considered in employer affirmative defense to sex harassment cases); *Montero v. AGCO Corp.*, 80 FEP Cases 1658 (9th Cir. 1999)(no claim for sex harassment under Title VII due to fact that employer promptly investigated and took action within 11 days of initial complaint).

carefully document its investigation and any action taken.

Another potential issue regards complaints of safety problems. Employers are obligated under the "general duty clause" of the Occupational Safety and Health Act to provide a workplace "free from recognized hazards that are likely to cause death or serious physical harm" to employees.[27] An employer who has knowledge of a preventable hazard and fails to correct it violates this obligation and is liable under the Act.[28] Therefore an employer who learns of a dangerous condition through an employee opinion survey is obligated under the general duty clause to make the workplace free from that condition.

Employee opinion surveys are not a panacea. Like any other employee relations tool, the survey must be part of a comprehensive employee relations strategy. Nevertheless, opinion surveys can form the backbone of a highly effective employee relations program. Surveys publicly demonstrate management's commitment to employee communication. They help pinpoint problem areas for attack, and they give companies an effective means of objectively judging the progress (or lack of progress) made on employee relations issues.

---

[27] 29 U.S.C. § 654.
[28] See *e.g. Pratt & Whitney Aircraft v. Secretary of Labor*, 649 F.2d 96 (2nd Cir. 1981)(dangerous potential of condition must be actually known or generally recognized before employer is liable for violation of general duty obligation).

Chapter 6

Supervisors – Foundation for Your Success

"I've been married three times, so I've had lots of supervision."
Upton Sinclair, interviewed at age 85

What You'll Learn In This Chapter
- ❑ Why line-level supervision is the key to your successful employee relations program
- ❑ The three reasons that supervisors so often form a weak foundation
- ❑ What your supervisors and managers need to know about emotional intelligence
- ❑ Why high supervisory scores on your opinion survey may be masking a bigger problem
- ❑ How to change your promotion policies to ensure a successful supervisory team
- ❑ The key "soft-skills" to teach your supervisory team
- ❑ Why training your supervisors is not enough – how to build accountability into your program

Managers will almost instinctively agree that supervisors are vital to the success of companies. The difficulty is that most managers never think further than the platitude. The unfortunate fact in most of the companies that I work with is that the most important link in the employee relations chain is given the least amount of attention; that is the job of the line level supervisor.

Companies often face many challenges with their supervisory group. In most companies the line level supervisor is the least appreciated and often most difficult job. Regularly companies will promote their best operators to become line level supervisors without considering whether these individuals have the skills to be an effective supervisor or equipping them with those skills. These companies lose their most productive operators and gain their worst supervisors with the same move.

This chapter briefly analyzes why the line level supervisor is such a vital position in the company and the foundation on which any successful employee relations project will stand. Second, it identifies why supervisors are often the weak link in a company's employee relations program. Finally it identifies some strategies to strengthen the foundation to your employee relations program.

Why Supervisors Are So Important
Managers often fail to consider the specific reasons why line level supervisors are vital to any successful employee relations effort. The reason that supervisors are so important is because they are closest to the daily action. Line level supervisors are in the best position to   identify operational problems, to make adjustments "on the fly" to insure that the operation runs smoothly, and to catch and dispel rumors in the organization. Line level supervisors have the most opportunities to communicate the company's vision. They are truly the "face" of everything that an organization does.

Additionally, supervisors play a vital "buffer" role between top management and production employees. Line level supervisors normally are individuals who most recently worked as operations employees. They often are close friends with the individuals who they now supervise. While this does create challenges for a new supervisor, it also creates a significant opportunities. Because of their close relationships with operations employees, line level supervisors are often less likely to be perceived on the "other side of the wall." For this reason they can be management's most effective voice for communicating the reasons for changes and for communicating the company's vision.

Finally, supervisors are vital to the company because this is typically where future leadership comes from. The skills and abilities developed in the supervisory group will become used by the future leaders of the company. If these skills are not cultivated in supervisors, one can rest assured that the future top management of the company will not suddenly become enlightened upon their promotion. Setting the example for the culture early in the leadership development process ensures that the "Leadership DNA" gets replicated throughout the management structure of the company.

Why Supervisors Often Form A Weak Foundation

In companies that we work with, we regularly find supervision is weak and ill prepared for their employee relations role in the company. There are a number of reasons that we have found that companies allow this to happen.

The first, and perhaps most common, reason is that line level supervisors have tremendously difficult jobs. They are "where the rubber meets the road" with respect to production issues. For that reason, line level supervisors are under constant pressure to produce the numbers. Since there is often very little attention paid to performance management issues there is much less pressure on supervisors to deliver in this area. The supervisors, logically enough, expend effort and increase skill level in areas where they are being watched more carefully.

Conversely, there is usually very little attention paid to performance management or "soft skills" of supervisors. New companies, and almost every company we work with, pay very little attention to the "emotional intelligence" skills of its leadership. These skills are rarely discussed by managers and supervisors.

Most companies feel like they have done a tremendous job in this area if they do as much as send managers and supervisors to a seminar or a course on introductory management and supervisory skills. Unfortunately, given the pressures on production outlined above, managers and supervisors are simply not asked to use the skills they learn and they become rusty and rarely, if ever, utilized.

Developing "Emotional Intelligence"

In the last several years a considerable amount has been written about "emotional intelligence" and its importance in predicting success of leaders. The theory was originally articulated by professors Peter Salovey and John Mayer and famously communicated by professor Daniel Goleman in his groundbreaking text *Emotional Intelligence*.

Goleman explains what many people know intuitively; "intelligence" is a poor predictor of success. He argues that what we have come to know as "intelligence" describes "intellectual intelligence" and is less likely to predict an individual's success than a set of skills and abilities that an individual uses when interacting with others, called "emotional intelligence."[29]

Emotional intelligence refers to the ability of a person to monitor and regulate one's own and other's feelings. In addition it describes a person's ability to use feelings to guide thought and action. Goleman identifies five emotional competencies that are most important indicators of emotional intelligence[30]: Self–awareness; Self-regulation; Motivation; Empathy; Social Skills.

In a number of studies conducted by Goleman and others, they estimate that while higher levels of technical competence is evident in roughly a quarter of "star" performers, the emotional competencies listed above were evident in over half of the "star" performers.[31] These findings have significant implications for training and development of supervisors and leaders in organizations.

First, the technical capabilities of a supervisor are really not that important. Most critical are their abilities to be aware and control their emotions, and use those skills to relate to and motivate those around them. Teaching technical "tools" to supervisors (and non-supervisors for that matter) is less important than helping them to hone their skills at dealing with emotions at work.

This is much harder work than simply sending someone to a class on performance management. It requires an individual to commit to a serious analysis of strengths and weaknesses regarding his emotional state at work (self-awareness) and developing skills to "close the gap" between his current emotional state

[29] *See Working with Emotional Intelligence*, (Bantam Books, 1988) pp.317-320.
[30] *Id.* p. 318.
[31] *Id.* pp.319-321.

and the desired state (self-regulation). It requires individuals to pay careful attention to the emotions of others and to take them into account when interacting with them (empathy and social skills).

Making these changes are not easy – while there will be breakthroughs there will be huge challenges, requiring motivation on the part of the individual supervisor. The good news is that Goleman's research, as well as the research of many others, concludes that these skills can be cultivated in individuals. As you begin to think about how you will develop your current supervisory group or candidates for upcoming supervisory positions, make certain to take time to look at ways to develop emotional intelligence competencies.

In addition, there are often no rewards for successful management of employee relations. Many companies, in fact, encourage poor supervisory and management skills by heaping rewards onto supervisors who "hit their numbers" even if their management style is threatening and abusive. In these companies the message sent by top management is that production is valued over the human experience of working for the company.

Employees in these companies see that management rewards the most negative example of supervision; supervisors see the example to which they should aspire if they too wish to be rewarded in the company. Even in companies where a high performing supervisor is disciplined for his or her efforts on employee relations, this is often done with a "wink" and the understanding that management is still very happy with the results.

Finally supervisors, like all humans, attempt to avoid pain. The fact is that performance related discussions and performance management are very difficult. Honestly confronting an employee with poor performance is hard. Most managers prefer to take the path of least resistance. This means either avoiding the performance discussion altogether or deflecting responsibility for the conversation some other direction.

For example, supervisors might say, "my boss told me that I have to tell you this..." or "this will never work, but top management wants us to try this." In this way the supervisor can avoid the negative experience of taking responsibility or defending the decision and at the same time show "empathy" with the worker who is being supervised.

Unfortunately, this hurts the company in the long run. Many companies we survey have discordant supervisory and top management scores. For example, immediate supervision scores may be relatively high whereas the top management scores will be extremely negative. Supervisors in these companies will often point to these scores as proof that they are doing a good job and that it is, "all their fault."

The point that they fail to realize is that the root cause of these scores is often the fact that supervisors refuse to take responsibility for their role as managers. One would expect top management to get hammered by a group of employees who are constantly being told by their immediate supervisor (also a member of management in their eyes) that the "top management" in the company is screwed up.

How To Strengthen The Foundation
The first step in strengthening the foundation of your supervisory group is to do a good job of promoting.

While there are a number of things a company can do to help improve the skills of a current group of supervisors, perhaps the most critical step to take is to promote individuals whose natural skill set is more in line with those required to be an effective supervisor.

There are some individuals who, no matter how much time and energy you invest in training and developing, will never be effective as supervisors. A company can save itself, and more importantly its employees, a considerable amount of grief by not promoting individuals into supervisory positions when they do not have the skills for that promotion.

While it sounds like common sense, this is the step most often overlooked by companies in the promotion process. There is a tremendous amount of pressure to promote the best performer or longer-term employees to become supervisors. This is the path of least resistance, but often a dead end.

The individuals that have seniority and are high performers must also be able to prove that they have the skill set necessary to be an effective supervisor. If they do not, then the task is to develop them in these areas <u>before</u> making a decision to promote. If this is your mindset, the quality of your supervisory team will improve automatically without the need for considerable work on the back end for development and training.

The key question is who should you be promoting? What skills and abilities should you look for when identifying potentially strong supervisors? While this is somewhat of an art over a science, there are a number of very good predictors of effective supervision skills. There are a number of assessments that are available to help identify individuals with strong skill sets. You can also informally watch your potential group of supervisory candidates for evidence of some of the same skills.

The most important skills to look for fall into the following categories:

- **Team orientation**: Look for individuals who are geared toward sharing information and working together as a team. An individual with a higher level of skill in this area is also effective in identifying the types of project where a team can be effective as well as the types of projects that are not going to be effectively solved by teams.

- **Influence skills**: Effective supervisors are good at influencing team members into taking action that is most consistent with the values and results expected of the organization. They will have high level communication capabilities and be effective at communicating both positive and constructive or negative information to their team members.

- **Initiative**: Look for individuals who are proactive and seek opportunities to take action that will avoid potentially bigger problems in the future. These individuals will also be on the lookout for potential problem performance areas and begin coaching in those areas well before an issue becomes a discipline problem.

- **Analysis and problem solving**: Good supervisors are excellent problem solvers and capable of analyzing complicated problems and coming up with effective solutions.   This will often happen under high pressure situations.

- **Situational style of interaction**: Finally, good supervisors are effective at knowing when to assume different roles as supervisor. This requires a heightened level of self-awareness, which is crucial to being a good supervisor. They can identify times when they need to be directive versus times when they need to be participative.

Since most companies have a larger supply of individuals interested in being promoted to supervisor than individuals who are naturally strong in all of the above listed skill sets, a program of training and developing non-supervisory employees should be established. If you know in advance the skill sets you are looking for in supervisors, it makes sense to ask your potential supervisory candidates to work on those skill areas as a prelude to being considered for a promotion.

This also gives you an opportunity to compare the various skill areas among potential supervisory candidates. Finally, it gives you an opportunity to develop "stretch" assignments and opportunities for candidates to get an opportunity to see them in action. This is one area where a proactive company can truly "try it before it buys it."

As a postscript, it is vitally important to remember that your highest producers may not be your best supervisors. While high producers do sometimes make effective supervisors, almost as often they do not. This is because a high producer who does not have good supervision skills is more likely to be a "working" supervisor and less likely to do an effective job at the actual day-to-day management of your human resources.

High producers will believe that they are doing an outstanding job of "supervising" due to the fact that they are able to continue to be high producers. If not directed regarding their roles and responsibilities as a manager, these individuals are very often the toughest to deal with since in their mind they continue to be valuable performers.

These problems are exclusively the responsibility of top management, who has done both a poor job of promoting and a poor job of explaining the responsibilities and expectations to its new line level supervisor. Unfortunately this is where most companies we work with live with respect to their promotions of supervisors.

What if your company is like most and has already promoted a number of supervisors who, while passable, do not have highly developed "soft skills"? Obviously your company will have to take steps to help train and develop these skills in your current supervisors. There are really two issues that must be considered. First, the company must offer skill development opportunities either on site or in the community. Second, the company must regularly stress the importance of these skills and hold supervisors and managers accountable for developing in these areas.

Most communities have a number of options when it comes to training and development. Local colleges or community colleges offer a wide number of classes on the subject. There are also a number of national organizations that host seminars regularly at convenient locations around the country. Many consulting firms (including ours) also offer on site skill development in these areas. Finally, there are a number of other options for even the most remote locations including training over the internet as well as videos and books on the subject. Getting high quality training is really much less of an issue than following up and applying the knowledge gained.

Most supervisors will tell you that they know what to do, but their challenge is doing it under fire. This is where the rubber meets the road with respect to soft skills and supervisory development. Supervisors must be required to use the skills that they have learned on a consistent basis. It is only by applying the concepts that they will eventually become second nature. There are a number of strategies that any firm can employ to help ensure the application of the concepts learned in training.

One important way to ensure communication skills are being used is by making line level supervisors responsible for the communication of important management information. Many companies will cut line level supervision out of the communication process for a number of reasons. They believe the line level supervisors will do a poor job of communicating the information or communicate the information inconsistently.

Many companies believe that it is easier to have one person, often the plant manager, tell everybody in one big meeting what it is they want the plant to know. While this method does have the advantage of consistency, it is perhaps the least effective method of ensuring that a message is properly received by employees. There are often way too many distractions during large group meetings. Employees are often intimidated or afraid to ask questions in such sessions. Other employees cut up and distract during these large group meetings. They become unwieldy and are too often an ineffective means of communicating.

Instead of avoiding the use of immediate supervisors in the communication process due to fears of their ability, these should be viewed as opportunities to train them in their communication skills. Using some of the strategies outlined in this book (arming line level supervisors with consistent information like a check list, outline, or a PowerPoint presentation; assigning higher level managers to attend meetings; holding follow-up focus group sessions to ensure that the message is being received as intended) a company need not worry that its message is not well communicated.

By strengthening the line level supervisor's role in the communication process the company helps ensure that supervisors are capable of answering questions from their employees. They also help supervisors feel more like a part of the management team. Most important, supervisors will know exactly what the rules are. It becomes very difficult for a supervisor to deny knowledge of a particular rule when they were responsible for the communication of that rule to their own employees.

Coaching skills and performance management can also be taught in the same fashion. Line level supervisors and managers should be held accountable for performance coaching of their direct reports. This can be done by requiring supervisors to hold performance discussion meetings with employees on a regular basis and to review a performance discussion planning form with their supervisor prior to any discussions.

Part of a supervisor's yearly review should include a review of performance discussion forms filled out during the year. A quick review of the personnel files of the supervisor's direct reports would give a reviewing manager a good idea of whether or not the company's performance management requirements are being met. These reviews, in order to be effective, should ideally occur several times a year or perhaps quarterly.

Supervisors and managers can be reviewed on team building and initiative skills in a number of ways. Informally this can be done during the quarterly review process where a supervisor is asked to describe anecdotally issues that have been solved by employee teams during that quarter. More formally, many firms employ 360-degree feedback wherein a supervisor's direct reports are asked to rate that supervisor on things like team orientation and initiative.

Ultimately if a company intends for employee relations skills to be a strength in its company, it must reward those skills. The bottom line is that if a supervisor achieves great results using less than satisfactory people skills, that supervisor should not receive higher rewards than less productive supervisors who do a good job at the "soft skills" area. Think of it like this: you literally get what you pay for with respect to performance management and coaching skills. If you do not reward these areas in your compensation system, you cannot expect them to be utilized by supervisors. It is just that simple.

The energy invested in developing supervisors and managers pays huge dividends. It improves employee relations by increasing communication with employees about things that are important to them. It improves the management team by building bench strength in the area of employee relations skills. It improves productivity and profitability because employees are better informed and more aware of the company's expectations and goals.

While there are a number of actions that your company may take before it begins to focus on supervisory development, there will be no action the company will take that will be more important to the employee relations environment in your company than improving supervisory skills.

Chapter 7

Communication Strategies for Policies, Procedures, Benefits and Compensation

The following are the universally fundamental laws of literary communication: 1. one must have something to communicate; 2. one must have someone to whom to communicate it; 3. one must really communicate it, not merely express it for oneself alone. Otherwise it would be more to the point to remain silent.
Friedrich Von Schlegel, German philosopher.

What we've got here is a failure to communicate.
Captain, Road Prison 36 (Strother Martin), in Cool Hand
Luke

What You'll Learn In This Chapter
- Some key principles of effective communication: consistency, clarity, multiple channels
- How to <u>use</u> the grapevine instead of fighting it
- Testing your communication program
- Why over-communicating is your goal
- Application of the principles to the examples of communicating about polices, procedures, benefits and compensation issues
- Handling communication of bad news

Almost every company we work with has trouble communicating with its workers. Employees turn to outside third parties because they feel they are not being heard or, worse, they believe they are being ignored. Companies with these problems must analyze two distinct issues:

- How do we currently communicate important information to our employees?
- How do our employees perceive the communication process?

The first step is to examine the fundamental communication process in the company. The company must identify whether it is consistently informing employees regarding important issues about their jobs. If important information is not being communicated, a system must be implemented to remedy this situation. The second step is to fight the battle of perception. Even if a company feels like it regularly communicates with its employees, if employees do not perceive this communication remains a problem and this perception must be dealt with. Each problem must be dealt with independently.

Before discussing specific issues common to organizations with employees who identify communication as a problem, we should first examine some basic principles of employee communication. These principles can be applied regardless of the particular message being communicated. The themes will be repeated as we apply them to two specific problems.

Consistent Message
One common problem with communication in organizations is inconsistency of the message. This can manifest itself in many different ways. For example, top management may deliver one message while line supervision gives another. Written communication may transmit a third message; from the grapevine, outside vendors or other sources there may be a fourth message. When bombarded by inconsistent messages, there is very little an employee

can do besides become confused. This confusion is automatically blamed on management, because they are expected to have a consistent message.

For this reason, it is very important that all messages from management be assessed as to their consistency with other communications. Top management, supervisors and outside vendors (who normally get their information from top management or supervisors) are certainly within the control of management and their messages must always be consistent. When the grapevine or other outside sources create inconsistencies in the message, it is important for management to correct those inconsistencies.

Only by creating consistent messages will employees be able to trust messages from management. Over a period of time, and with strict attention paid to matters of communication, management will become a trusted source for information. This can be a lengthy process, particularly after a union organizing campaign or other upheaval. It takes a significant period of time and consistency for employees to regain this trust.

Keep It Simple
Another very important aspect of employee communication is to keep messages simple, even when complex information must be communicated. Test messages and communication pieces in focus groups of either supervisors or employees. Ensure that the message the company is trying to communicate is clearly understood. Try to break messages into small component parts and communicate each component of the message clearly and effectively.

Communication today is much different than in the past. Compare the popular methods of communication in today's society with those of years ago. Long written letters and extensive verbiage are almost never used in today's communication environment. This is a time of sound bites, short e-mail messages and lots of visual messages. Advertising campaigns are a good source of learning about communication. Some of the most famous are one-and two-word campaigns (Got Milk?). The vast majority of the country gets information from *USA Today*, not the *New York Times*. Think of comic books versus *War and Peace*. The bottom line is that the success of any communication is if the receiver gets the message that the communicator wanted him to receive. The simpler the message, the more likely that will eventually occur.

Use as Many Senses as Possible

Make sure that messages are communicated in a way that involves as many senses as possible. People receive messages not only by reading words, but also seeing pictures, hearing, touching and even smelling. It is important to reach as many of these senses as possible in your communications. When training an employee in a particular task, do not rely solely on written words describing how to do the process. You should also include a spoken training session and give employees an opportunity to perform the task physically. By using different approaches, you have ensured that no matter what primary method of learning and receiving messages an employee may prefer, your attempt to communicate the message has hit that communication style.

Multiple Channels

Make sure that each message is communicated through a variety of different channels. Companies that post messages on bulletin boards and assume the message is communicated are typically the types of companies whose problems end up on our desks. Also, assuming that employees receive a message simply because someone has been told to communicate the message is a mistake and, frankly, inept management. Instead, any message needing to be communicated must be distributed through as many channels as exist in the company.

Communicating through multiple channels creates multiple "impressions" of the same message. Consider the example of studying for an exam in school. Most people are not able to study for a school exam by merely reading the text once. Often students re-read the same text several times. They may even take notes or create flash cards to help them study. Some students not only attend lectures, but also record them so they can listen to them again later. This is a way to create multiple impressions of the same material.

Advertising agencies use the same theory. Companies do not buy one ad and then stop. They will often buy several months or even years of ad space. They will coordinate messages on TV with messages in magazines, newspapers and radio. In this way, through multiple impressions, advertising agencies make sure that a consistent message is communicated and received by the public.

To have a successful communication strategy in your company, make sure to have multiple impressions of the same message distributed across as many channels as possible. A few examples of effective means of distribution (and this is certainly not an exhaustive list) are:

- Print – bulletin board postings, paycheck stuffers, memos, signs in the break room, etc.
- Auditory – team meetings, broadcast over loud speaker, audio tape, quarterly meetings, etc.
- Electronic – e-mail, company intranet, video tape, PowerPoint slides, etc.

The Grapevine

When deciding how to communicate a message, consider all the ways employees receive messages in your company. One method mentioned before, but worth repeating, is the grapevine. Many companies allow the grapevine to become their downfall, either by ignoring or failing to correct rumors or pretending that the grapevine does not exist.

Every business has informal networks of employees who communicate on a daily basis. Have you ever hung out with the smokers in your company (if you are one, you know exactly what I mean)? In fact, surveys indicate that the grapevine is often the number one source of information for many employees. Do not ignore the fact that the grapevine exists; learn to use it as a method to communicate messages. If management is not managing the grapevine, it is allowing the grapevine to manage the communication of its messages.

Informal network leaders should be used as sounding boards for communication of important messages and management should test whether these informal leaders have received the message that management intends to convey. In addition, when the grapevine is communicating false information, it is critical for management to immediately attack that misinformation. The company must then reinforce the correct information to ensure consistency of the company message is maintained in that communication channel. While there is no way to stop all misinformation flowing through the grapevine, management must always consider this channel when dealing with its communication strategies.

Test Your Success

One often-ignored aspect of communication strategy is determining whether or not the message has actually been communicated. After communicating an important message to employees, it is a good practice to conduct some sampling to discover if the message has been communicated in a consistent fashion and has been clearly understood by employees. This sampling can include formal focus groups or informal interviews with employees.

The best time to sample is after a little time has elapsed from the initial communication of the message. This is the only way to ensure that the message has been communicated properly and, most important, it counts as another impression for purposes of communication strategy.

Isn't This Over-Communicating?

When we work with companies, particularly ones that have done a poor job of communicating in the past, a question often asked is "isn't this over-communicating?" The answer is yes. Over-communicating is a critical strategy for companies with communication problems. There are a couple of reasons companies with communication problems should respond by over-communicating.

First, these businesses must learn how to communicate. A lot of time and effort should be devoted, particularly in the early stages of revamping communication capabilities, in assessing whether messages have been communicated through as many channels as possible and actually received and understood by the employees.

Second, over-communication is an intentional strategy to overcome the perception that a company is not communicating well. A large increase in the number of impressions of company messages will be perceived as a change for the better in the company.

This is especially important on the heels of a union organizing campaign. Most companies communicate more regularly and more effectively during a union campaign than they ever have before. If the company goes back to its normal pattern of communication after the campaign employees will sense a huge vacuum of information flow. This jeopardizes relationships built during the campaign and feeds claims by union supporters that the company's interest in employees during the campaign was simply a tactic and that no improvements will be made. Without public evidence to the contrary these claims can be very persuasive.

While employees may at first feel bombarded by the number of messages directed to them, they will form the distinct feeling that management is trying, (maybe even trying too hard), to ensure they are receiving the information needed to effectively do their jobs. While eventually management can back off from this approach, in the early stages the overload of information is critical. In addition, this strategy gives management the opportunity to test as many different communication methods as possible in the only environment that matters – their own.

Methods of communication work differently in each company. Every business is unique and requires its own system for communicating messages. By experimenting with as many different methods of communicating as possible, management can evaluate which methods are most effective in its particular company and then rely more heavily on those methods in the future.

Don't Forget Humor

People remember something that is funny, so humor is a good tool to add to your employee communication toolkit. Particularly in companies that have gone through serious upheavals in the recent past, it is important to lighten things up as much as possible. Humor is a good way to achieve that end. The inclusion of topical cartoons and humorous messages as part of a communication program can assure retention of the message and also help to reduce tension provoked by tough issues. Using these strategies effectively can defuse what might be considered a seriously negative employee relations problem in an at-risk business.

Client Story: Intentional Non-Communication?

During union organizing campaigns, companies are regularly hit with unfair labor practice charges. These charges are often used strategically by unions to create the impression that companies are "bad actors" deserving of a union. This is not to say that unfair labor practice charges do not occur during organizing campaigns, but experience shows that the vast majority of these charges are subsequently dropped by the union or not pursued by the National Labor Relations Board. A large portion of those that remain are settled by the NLRB.

Companies that settle unfair labor practices are often asked to post a notice stating they will refrain from committing unfair labor practices in the future. This is one case where the company's poor communication methods of the past can actually work to its advantage. I have regularly heard business owners protest, "I'm not posting a notice - they are making me look like a criminal in my own work place." I would then calmly walk them by the company bulletin board (where such notices would be posted) and point out to them the now aged-stained and faded memos from years gone by posted on the same bulletin board. "When was the last time you looked at this bulletin board?" I would ask. "If I wanted to make sure no one read something, this is exactly where I would post it.

In fact, during one hotly contested campaign we were asked by the National Labor Relations Board to issue a memo to all employees of the company. When asked how to distribute the information, we were told to do so through normal channels. In that particular case our "normal" channels had worked dismally in communicating just about every other important message over the prior year. That woefully ineffective method was an "all hands" memo stacked in the employee break room. While typically a terrific source of scrap paper for employees, these memos were almost never read and essentially created a litter problem.

Therefore, we dutifully distributed the memos by stacking them in the employee break room. Weeks later stacks of memos (the ones that had not already been thrown in the trash) remained right where they were originally placed. "Communication" accomplished.

Application of Strategies – Two Particular Problems

Policies and Procedures

One of the most common areas where employers communicate poorly with employees is on issues concerning policies and procedures. A common complaint among employees is that policies and procedures are unfairly administered. Often this claim of "unfair administration" has two core components. Supervisors may, in fact, be applying rules inconsistently due to their own misunderstanding of policies and procedures in the company. The second, and equally important component, is that employees do not fully understand the company's policies and procedures. Both of these problems are communication issues.

When it comes to communicating policies and procedures, the first step the employer must take is to ensure that its policies and procedures are organized in such a way that they can be communicated effectively. These messages must be organized logically and convey relevant information in clear language. A review of the employer's policies and procedures manual should be undertaken with an eye to these qualities. Where weaknesses exist, these materials must be revised.

What's the Difference Between an Employee Handbook and a Policy Manual?

Company managers and supervisors are often confused about the distinction between policy manuals and employee handbooks. For those businesses that have both, each serves an independent purpose.

The purpose of an employee handbook is to communicate to line level employees the general policies and procedures they need to know to be effective in the company. The handbook may include summaries of important rules, benefits and pay, disciplinary procedures and other "everyday" information. These handbooks are typically written in an easy-to-understand form and are not necessarily comprehensive. Not every policy or procedure will be included in an employee handbook. Neither will every detail of the policy and procedures summarized in the handbook be included.

A policy and procedure manual, on the other hand, is a more detailed guide for supervisors or managers. This reference is used in day-to-day implementation of policy and procedures during the course of their work. These manuals give more detailed descriptions of procedures, often including examples of how to apply policies and procedures under various factual situations. They are, by their very nature, much more comprehensive and "legalistic."

For example, a handbook provision about vacations might outline briefly the fact that vacations are provided to employees as a benefit of employment and delineate the number of weeks of vacation awarded to employees for various years of service. This handbook provision might also include a sentence explaining that the administration of vacations is handled according to a vacation policy. Employees would then be directed to ask questions about the administration of that policy to their immediate supervisors.

A policy and procedure covering vacations, on the other hand, would include more extensive guidelines regarding administration of vacation: how vacation is requested, whether or not it can be carried over, what happens if a holiday falls during a vacation and a host of other issues that arise concerning vacation policy. Some companies will include more information in employee handbooks than others. A good rule of thumb is to include information answering common issues among employees in the application of the policy and procedure. Handbook information should answer most questions, while at the same time be short and concise.

For an example of sample handbook and policy statements, see Appendix 3.

When considering communicating policies and procedures to employees, a number of communication channels should be considered. The first channel is, of course, the language of the handbook or policy and procedure itself. These should be reviewed on a regular basis, not only for their legality, but also for their ability to communicate effectively.

Handbooks should be kept as simple as possible, since they have the broadest distribution and will be relied on most regularly by employees. Policies and procedures, while more detailed, should also be reviewed for ease of administration and understanding by supervisors.

Consider asking focus groups of employees and supervisors to review policies. Ask them whether they understand the documents. Ask them how they would apply the policy to hypothetical situations. Once satisfied with the language, handbooks and policy manuals should be printed and distributed to employees. The employer should also consider including policies and procedures and employee handbooks online if the company has an intranet.

Other channels of communication also should be explored. The orientation process, for example, should be examined with respect to how effectively policies, procedures and handbooks are explained during that session. Video presentations or multimedia computer sessions on the handbook are excellent tools for creating another "impression" on the policy and procedure issue. These tools can also be used later for retraining purposes.

To create another impression, training sessions on policies and procedures should also be considered. These sessions can be held with groups of supervisors. Discussion should focus on the application of policies to ensure they are administered fairly and consistently. Sessions can also be held with hourly employees to make sure that they understand the exact rules and conditions surrounding a particular policy and procedure. Most important, employees need to be informed of the reasons for various policies and procedures.

These sessions are not designed to cover all policies and procedures in a comprehensive fashion. A better plan is to choose bite size issues, each handled in its own session. Employers could, for example, rotate regular employees through the employee orientation process. This practice can serve several purposes. It gives current employees an opportunity to review the orientation process for possible changes and improvements the company can make to get new employees up to speed. It also creates an additional impression on policies and procedures, along with the other issues covered in orientation. Finally, this process will involve employees in the development of training in an area in which they have significant expertise – their own jobs.

Another possible communication strategy surrounding policies, procedures or handbook provisions is using bulletin board posters, paycheck stuffers, memos, and articles in company newsletters covering a particular policy or procedure that has generated confusion or problems.

Finally, supervisors should be trained to manage the grapevine regarding policy and procedures issues. This requires that they be thoroughly familiar with various policies, procedures and handbook provisions. In addition, they should be trained to correct improper statements they overhear regarding company procedures.

Supervisors will often hear conversations where employees are complaining about the unfairness of a particular policy or procedure. Supervisors and managers must be alert to these complaints. They must take these opportunities to communicate the reasons for company policies, the company's commitment to fairly and consistently apply those policies across work groups and, if a complaint appears to have some validity, to ensure that the company investigates the issue in question. It is critical that employees receive feedback from the supervisor about any promised investigation.

Compensation and Benefits
This is another area where employers create huge problems in the workforce because of inept communication strategies. Pay and benefits are essential issues to all employees. These issues are regularly rated low in employee opinion surveys we conduct, particularly in companies that have been

through union organizing campaigns. This occurs in part due to unrealistic promises made by union organizers during campaigns, but more regularly it is a result of the fact that employees have their own unrealistic views about pay and benefit compensation in the overall market.

Employees frequently do not understand how pay is administered and automatically assume that it is done in an unfair or haphazard fashion. It is vitally important for companies to regularly communicate to employees about their pay and benefit packages and to explain how they are developed and administered. This, of course, presupposes that an employer's wage and benefit policies and procedures are fairly administered, a subject that is dealt with in another chapter.

Communicating pay and benefits issues should also be considered a continuing process. There are, again, several options to consider. The first place to start is to examine the current pay and benefit policies and whatever communication material presently exists. The explanatory material should be simple to understand summaries of the employer's pay system. The communication should be delivered by memo or flier and should describe the complete process.

The flier or brochure should explain the principles behind the pay and benefit plan. It might explain, for example, that the company wishes to pay in the top third of the market for the various jobs that exist in its market. A second comment should explain how the company administers that philosophy. This could include explanations regarding the types of wage and salary reviews conducted, the geographic areas and industries reviewed, and the like. The piece might then describe a yearly review process to make sure that wage ranges are within market rates and comply with the company's philosophy on pay. Finally, the piece should include examples of how the pay policy is actually administered to employees.

This type of communication can be used in the recruiting, hiring and orientation processes, and even as a follow-up or retraining piece to be used during supervisory meetings regarding pay and benefits. The information can also be used during the yearly appraisal process. In addition to the printed communication, a company should also consider providing a training session on pay and benefits. Again, this could be included as part of the orientation process and then subsequently used in retraining sessions for supervisors and managers. If groups of employees have questions about the pay system, this training session could be available in that process.

In addition, particularly with respect to issues of pay and benefits that are very important and potentially negative issues with employees, the use of individualized employee meetings should be considered. Individual supervisors should be trained to discuss the company's pay principles and procedures with employees during the appraisal process and any other time that there are questions. Our experience is that individualized meetings regarding these issues help to defuse potentially negative situations (see "Being the Bearer of Bad News," below). These meetings also help avoid some of the potentially touchy mass negativism that can occur during group sessions over these highly personal issues. Individual meetings, of course, can also become negative and it is important to train supervisors to effectively deal with these situations.

Another popular communications strategy is the "total compensation communication" used in many businesses today. Companies that use this strategy create a statement that can be used either as a paycheck stuffer or voiced in separate individual meetings. This statement analyzes an employee's total compensation, including taxes paid by the employer on behalf of the employee, cost of benefits, cost of vacation and holiday pay, etc. This statement can, in its best form, graphically illustrate to the employee significant amounts of compensation that are often lost "through the cracks." The information also indicates to employees that their compensation is significantly more than what they normally believe to be the case. An important point to remember about this and any other communication strategy is that, standing alone, it is insignificant. Any piece must be part of an overall communication strategy on the compensation and benefits issue.

Being the Bearer of Bad News
An important part of every management team's communication strategy includes dealing effectively with bad news. The natural reaction for most people, whether at work or at home, is to avoid uncomfortable situations or conflicts. These are unfortunately common occurrences in a workplace setting and, if avoided, can lead to misunderstandings and hurt feelings. In extreme cases these situations can lead to union campaigns.

Handling bad news is something of an art form. However, a number of principles can be used to ease the situation. First, you must avoid "beating around the bush" when it comes to communicating bad news. Most people see hesitation as avoiding responsibility for dealing with issues and as an exhibition of a lack of strength or leadership. Second, consistency of communication is crucial during a period when bad news is being communicated. Whether the issue is a layoff, an increase in benefit costs, a termination, or other serious incident, managers and supervisors must develop a consistent message to employees and develop a united front. Dealing effectively with negative situations demonstrates leadership and increases respect for managers and supervisors.

As discussed earlier, a common paradox occurs in employee opinion surveys we have conducted in companies that have recently been through organizing campaigns. That paradox is that immediate supervisors typically rate much higher than top management. Supervisors often point to this as redemption for them (i.e. "top management was the problem all along"). Upon closer analysis, we regularly learn that this is not the case and that the issue is more likely a communication problem.

It is more often the case that supervisors, siding with their employees and against management, refuse to take responsibility for negative news. These actions reveal a lack of leadership and it leads employees to believe their complaints are legitimate. Employees will take the fact that their supervisor agrees with them as validation of their complaint against top management. While occasionally the supervisors are right – top management is the problem – more often, supervisors will just agree with employee complaints as the path of least resistance.

Supervisors must not take part in disparaging the company and should take responsibility for explaining the company's reasons for taking action. Employees do not have to agree with everything the company does, but if they understand the process behind the company's decisions and that their welfare is a top priority for the company, they will be more likely to listen. Employees must also understand that, as in any business, business health must be considered for the overall welfare of the company, which ultimately affects the welfare of all employees. In this way, an effective communication strategy to deliver bad news can actually create desirable results.

Client Story: Bearing Bad Benefit News

One company we helped was nearing the end of their "certification year," about 12 months after narrowly defeating a union election. The last election, which occurred directly after a poorly communicated benefit change and rollout, was attributed in part to that negative information. Over the course of the ensuing year, the company made great strides in many areas, and conducted a second employee opinion survey just prior to announcing benefits changes again. That survey showed that employee satisfaction had increased dramatically.

However, just weeks before the benefit announcement and, unfortunately, also weeks before the union could file another petition, the company received horrible news. The benefits plan that had created so much anguish the year before was now going to have, on average, a 25% premium increase for employees. The company was not in a financial position at the time to absorb much, if any, of the increased benefit cost. This was indeed a gray day.

After absorbing the news, the management team went to work. They had made significant gains with employees over the course of the year and had built up an increased level of trust. Management had gained experience communicating on a variety of workplace issues during that year and employees had attested to positive changes that the company had made. In this environment, managers and supervisors met individually with employees.

Those meetings included several themes. First, managers and supervisors congratulated employees on the recent survey results while acknowledging that there was still work to do. Second, the managers and supervisors noted that they had news about the benefit program that, for a significant number of employees, was not good news.

Each supervisor was then prepared to discuss benefit options with each employee. The discussion included increased premium cost under the current plan, along with an explanation of other available plan options available that might reduce the benefit expenses for families.

Next, the supervisors and managers were directed to empathize with employees regarding the situation (which was not difficult since many of them were absorbing the same benefit cost increases). The meeting closed with an explanation to employees of the enrollment process and an opportunity to resolve any questions or issues they had regarding benefits.

Much to the company's surprise, the benefit rollout during this period was extremely smooth. Obviously, many employees were frustrated and there were negative comments regarding the increase in rates. Nevertheless, employees understood that the employer was truly between a rock and a hard place because supervisors had been educated about the various options the employer had considered and effectively shared this information. Employees understood this was an industry-wide phenomenon. Finally, supervisors explained that the company was looking at the issue as a total compensation issue. In

fact, employees witnessed several changes in compensation during the course of the year that were consistent with the employer's efforts to stay within market rates.

Honesty, empathy and individualized treatment on the issue defused what only a year before had been a core organizing issue.

Always Respond

The final lesson in communicating with employees is that you must always respond to employee requests. One of the most common complaints employees make regarding communication is that they ask their supervisors for information or have questions, and receive no response. There is no doubt that this is sometimes a perception problem on behalf of employees because it is very easy for employees to ignore supervisory feedback that is inconsistent with what they desire. At the same time, supervisors should make sure that they have a process in place to ensure that employee requests are responded to every time and handled in a timely manner.

The best way to implement this practice is to document employee requests and to respond to them in writing. While this can increase workload, it is a way to ensure that both the supervisor and the employee know that a response has been made. Not every request requires a formal response of this nature (and by formal we are not talking about long and carefully crafted letters – handwritten notes are fine) but verbal responses should be used only on the most routine issues. As mentioned before, for companies that have recently undergone organizing campaigns or that have problems with employees regarding perceived communication deficiencies, it is best to over-communicate in response to requests.

One strategy we have seen work is the use of 3x5 cards. When an employee makes a request on one of these cards it is routed through the company to the individual who can answer the question. The card is to be returned, with the answer from the appropriate person, no less than 24 hours from the time it is submitted. This practice is a simple and effective method for combating perceptions of supervisory aloofness or lack of empathy with employee problems.

Communication is a fundamental issue in almost every "at risk" company. Whatever strategies you decide to use, the key is to focus on whether the message has been received, not just on whether it has been delivered. The good news is that effort spent resolving this issue helps to resolve so many others. It is a foundation of good management and is a cornerstone to highly productive and satisfied work forces.

Chapter 8

Employee Involvement – A True Win-Win

I tell you and you forget. I show you and you remember.
I involve you and you understand.
Eric Butterworth

What You'll Learn In This Chapter
- ❏ When to use a team – and when <u>not</u> to use one
- ❏ Choosing the issue for a team
- ❏ Common causes for failed teams
- ❏ Examples of teams in action – safety and work conditions issues
- ❏ How to avoid the legal pitfalls that can be associated with the use of teams

Two common areas of frustration in the companies we survey are working conditions and workplace safety. These issues impact employees daily, and can become areas of intense frustration, and trigger great employer expense. Unions often take advantage of frustration surrounding these issues during organizing campaigns – employees surveyed at the conclusion of these campaigns regularly express continued dissatisfaction. While we never applaud employers with poor work conditions or safety problems, these issues provide excellent opportunities for quick, public wins. They are also excellent opportunities for employee involvement.

A Word About Teams
Team-based solutions are so regularly prescribed today they have become almost trite. Company leaders have often read (*ad nauseam*) about the advantages of team-oriented problem solving. Yet

many have tried to implement team-based solutions to deal with issues in their workplaces with no success.

One reason for this disconnect is that teams are often prescribed to solve problems that they are ill-suited to attack. Therefore, before determining whether or not to solve a problem using a team-based approach, a company must understand the strengths and weaknesses of teams.

Certain categories of problems are not suited for teams. At the same time, employee involvement can be a significant source of strength in other issues. Therefore, managers must first be able to identify opportunities for effective use of teams before designating a team to look at a particular problem.

Assigning a team to solve a problem that is not practical for employee involvement has two important negative impacts on a business. First, it discredits the team concept and reduces the likelihood that teams will be effectively used in areas where they should have strength.

A second problem is that using a team to solve a problem inappropriate for employee involvement de-motivates team members and discourages employees from getting involved. At its worst, a team-based experience can create tension and dissatisfaction among groups of employees. The table below describes the categories of problems best suited for team-based problem solving and those more appropriate for individual problem solving.

Team-Based Problem Solving	Individual Problem Solving
Complex issues, with few readily identifiable solutions	Readily identifiable solutions
Team members' areas of expertise could help identify solutions	Team members share little expertise
Limited or identifiable time line	Solution requires long-term and continued attention
Scientific analysis and measurement is possible	Analysis and measurement is difficult or impossible
Clearly identifiable end point or "finish line"	No readily identifiable end point

The selected project, particularly for a first team effort, should meet a number of criteria. It should not be a randomly selected project or one identified by a vote or other such process. It should be carefully selected for its ability to be resolved with a team-oriented approach. It is also important to select a project that has a direct impact on internal and/or external customers. This will ensure the project implementation will have a visible effect and thus can be experienced by employees not directly involved in the process.

The project should also be meaningful to employees. A project initiated to solve a minor issue or something generally perceived to be a "non-issue" among employees is not likely to generate much excitement about the team process. Employees may even feel that the company is just "tossing them a bone" or trying to mollify them when they are given unimportant problems to solve. Rather, pick a project that has the potential for showing measurable results or recycles daily or weekly. If the project is not measurable or the process does not occur on a regular basis, it is difficult to identify whether the team process has been successful or not.

A project that cuts across departments is better to tackle than one involving only one department. This not only increases the visibility of the project throughout the company, but it allows employees from different departments to work together toward a common goal, which is often out of the ordinary. This also gives employees from different departments time to experience some of the challenges different employees face in the company. This opportunity can create empathy and a new respect for the employees of different departments. It also provides fresh perspectives to problems that may have perplexed others in the past.

Finally, the project should not involve a process in transition. The process being dealt with should be well settled so that accurate data regarding the process and progress made by the team can be assessed. If it is a process in transition, there is little way to meaningfully measure results.

The Project
- Selected by management
- Direct impact on internal or external customers
- Meaningful to employees
- Measurable results or recycles daily or weekly
- Cuts across departments
- Not a process in transition

After identifying an issue that can be readily attacked by a group of employees, the next step is to select the employees to be part of the team assigned to the problem. Several issues should be considered when identifying people to participate in group problem solving. First, and most obvious, the individuals must be capable of working well with other people.

Employee involvement committees do not have to be made up of volunteers exclusively (which can be a disadvantage at times). However, participants should be open to the process of team-based problem solving.

Next, it is important that individuals chosen for the group have skills or expertise in the area being considered. For general problem solving on issues that impact the work force as a whole, finding employees with expertise will not be difficult. Particularized safety and work conditions issues, on the other hand, may require individuals in specialized job categories or outside consultants with relevant expertise. Some employers even go a step further and evaluate their workforce to discover hidden talents that might be brought to bear on a specific problem.

The individuals chosen should also be skilled at working together as a group. This is not the same thing as having a willingness to work together. Team-based solutions to problems require excellent meeting and brainstorming skills. Our first step when using focus groups or work teams is to regularly conduct generalized training on group problem-solving skills before dealing with specific issues. This process helps more experienced team members refresh their skills and allows other members access to a set of competencies to bring to future meetings.

Finally, as part of the employee relations aspect to team processing, choose good communicators and natural leaders from the company. Volunteers are not always the best way to obtain group members for a particular committee. Oftentimes it is better to hand pick team members based on a combination of factors. These are not necessarily the most popular or most positive employees in the company. It is very important, particularly if team-oriented solutions are either new to the company or negatively perceived due to problems in the past, to select employees who are leaders in the informal network of the organization. Committee members should be individuals who are respected for their objectivity and commitment to the business.

Once the issue has been picked and committee members chosen and trained, the next step is getting to work on the issue.

What Can Go wrong
Never ending teams
Unfocused teams
Teams focused on the wrong
    issues
Wrong people on teams
No follow-up
Poor leadership

Not all businesses can effectively use teams to implement responses to problems. Good predictors of whether or not a company will be able to use teams are the following:
- The company regularly shows a commitment to the customer and to continuous improvement.
- Employees have a clear understanding of their jobs and how they fit into the overall company.
- Employees feel their jobs are important, and they are committed to the overall success of the company.
- Employees understand their jobs are to work together to create a continuous flow of value-added tasks from the supplier to the customer.
- The use of hierarchy is diminished in this culture.
- Individual contributions are valued and employees are encouraged to act in their area of expertise.

- Data and information are accurate and used regularly in the decision-making process.
- The feedback of results and performance from customers to suppliers is regularly evaluated as part of the system.

This does not mean that companies that do not share all of these goals or fail to implement them effectively (often a symptom of companies who are having labor relations problems in the first place) will find it impossible to use teams. We have successfully assisted with the team process many companies whose business culture would not immediately meet the criteria listed here. However, companies that wish to use teams will want to push their business culture in the direction described above.

In order to successfully use a team process, there are several key principles to which companies must adhere. First, it is important to clearly define the goals, action plans, responsibilities and deadlines for the team. It is critical for team members to know how their efforts will be measured and when their goal should be accomplished; otherwise, it is impossible to know whether the team process has been a success or failure. It results in the team losing focus. The team should be able to regularly refer back to its action plans, goals and deadlines to keep its bearings.

The team members should communicate up and down the line regarding the progress of the team. In other words, the team should be communicating to people at its level and below regarding the information being collected and the process the team is undergoing to resolve the issues. The team should also be communicating above to managers, notifying them of progress made toward reaching the goals.

Keep the team together until the results are in. Disbanding a team before knowing whether or not its efforts were successful is problematic. First, the team loses the opportunity to celebrate its success – it is not enough to celebrate, "We worked together as a team!" There must be a moment where the team can collectively celebrate, "We worked together and this is what we accomplished." Second, and more important, if the project failed, the team loses the opportunity to make an honest assessment of its methods. Finally, it is critical to talk to the people affected by the team's decisions. Those people directly impacted should know and understand the recommendations of the team, measurements used to identify success or failure and the team's assessment of its results.

What Makes a Successful Team

- Clarity of goals
- Clearly defined roles and ground rules
- Clear communication
- Beneficial behavior by members
- Well defined decision procedures
- Balanced participation
- Use of a scientific approach

Failed teams share a number of common symptoms. The first area where teams fail is "floundering" or indecision over the next action to take. This problem arises when the team has not clearly established its goals and set deadlines. It is best resolved by going back to the initial team action planning and purpose statement and assessing what that plan requires the team to do next.

Another common problem with teams concerns the psychology of the participants. Overbearing or dominating members can derail the team process and trivialize others' opinions. Reluctant participants are the flip side of this problem. These people are either unable or unwilling to provide feedback or suggestions and do not contribute to overall team success.

If these two problems exist, bringing in a skilled facilitator can move the conversation forward. Facilitators are trained to reduce the impact of overbearing or dominating participants. For example, the facilitator may ask each participant to add a comment or suggestion, and thereby reduce the ability of the overbearing participants to "take over the floor." Facilitators can also effectively encourage reluctant participants and increase feedback and input from all members of the team.

Unquestioned acceptance of opinion as fact is another symptom of teams that fail. Team members must be properly trained to identify the difference between fact and opinion. The use of the scientific method of fact gathering is a critical aspect of the team process.

In order to effectively identify whether success has occurred, it is important to agree on terms of measurement and to make sure that the decisions made by the team are based on objective data and not simply opinion. Once again, a skilled facilitator can assist with forcing team members to examine information carefully, verify conclusions and identify areas where more data would be helpful in the process.

Some teams fail because they experience a rush to "accomplishment." This means that teams can often be misguided and ignore viable possibilities because they want to quickly show success on a particular issue. Again, a facilitator can serve a vital role in this situation by reminding team members to examine all possibilities and use a scientific process to identify whether the goals set are indeed the ones accomplished.

Finally, common characteristics of failing teams are problems of attribution, discounting contributions, tangents and feuds. Sometimes team members take individual credit for accomplishments of the team or divert attention from the specific goals or game plans identified at the beginning of the team process because of private agendas, jealousy or ill will. This can derail the progress of the team. Again, a skilled facilitator can keep the team focused on the problem to be solved.

Next we will look at how teams and employee involvement can work effectively on safety and work condition issues.

Safety Programs
There are several advantages to focusing on safety issues as an opportunity for employee involvement. Safety programs are well suited for team-based approaches to problem solving. They meet many of the criteria listed above for problems well suited for team-based approaches. Consider safety problems in the context of the types of these issues:

- **Complex problem with few readily identifiable solutions** – Safety problems often require significant investigation and analysis of how possible solutions will impact the performance of the company.
- **Problem where team members' areas have valuable expertise** – Safety issues are

particularly well-suited for employee input because employees are affected daily by decisions made regarding workplace safety. They typically have the best view of where safety problems arise and how particular solutions will impact the workers.

- **Problem with limited or identifiable timeline** – Many safety problems have readily identifiable end points, like a change in a procedure or process or addition of a safety feature. Other safety issues are continuing projects – an ergonomics program, for example. It is important to identify a project with a limited timeline if employee involvement is a goal.
- **Issue where scientific analysis and measurement is possible** – There are a multitude of opportunities to measure and scientifically evaluate both company history with respect to safety on particular issues, as well as the success of programs identified and adopted through an employee involvement process.
- **Direct impact on internal or external customers** – There are clearly direct impacts on internal customers – the employees directly affected by the safety program. Impacts on external customers are less visible, if they exist at all. Again, potential projects should be evaluated with consideration of their impact on customers in mind.
- **Meaningful to employees** – Probably no more meaningful projects are possible than those that directly impact the safety of employees.
- **Cuts across departments** – Depending on the safety program chosen, many programs will cut across departmental lines and can be exceptional projects for employee involvement.
- **Not a process and transition** – This is another area where potential safety projects will have

mixed results, depending on the nature of the project. It is best to choose a project where the process or procedure is in place and there is a measurable safety history to review.

Management should evaluate every project with an eye to these criteria, and pick a project which best meets these factors. Nevertheless, many safety projects meet most (if not all) of the criteria for effective team topics.

There are both advantages and disadvantages to choosing safety programs as employee involvement initiatives. The advantages are many. Employee safety programs, first and foremost, show compassion on the part of the employer and prove to employees that the employer takes employee welfare very seriously. During an employee involvement process regarding safety issues, managers are afforded many opportunities to exhibit this concern on the part of the employer. Companies also benefit through reductions in costs associated with insurance claims, workers compensation, absenteeism and lost time due to accidents.

Employees also benefit. Group participants are given the opportunity to communicate in small groups and even individually with managers to help create an understanding of important safety issues. They get to know their managers and co-workers better. They share safety tips and can warn the company of unsafe practices before they result in injury. Finally, if successful, they have the satisfaction of making their workplace safer.

Some disadvantages may be present when focusing on job safety programs, particularly if conducted as the first employee involvement program on the heels of the union organizing campaign. Safety issues are often used during organizing campaigns to inflame voters. Often unions will have employees file OSHA complaints to harass an employer during organizing drives. These complaints may still be pending at the conclusion of the NLRB election process.

In addition, safety rhetoric is well suited for inflammatory action by extremely negative employees. These employees will simply not effectively participate in a team or they may attempt to derail discussion by continuing inflammatory rhetoric. In this environment, employers are often best advised to avoid employee involvement on these particular issues.

This is not to say that the issues should be ignored. However, they may be best handled directly through management with limited employee involvement. These decisions, of course, are handled during the management evaluation of potential team projects. A careful issue selection process avoids creating additional issues in contentious areas that may already be subjects of agency inquiry.

Work Conditions
Work conditions issues are also well suited for employee involvement. Once again, they typically meet the criteria of good team-based projects:

• **Complex problem with few readily identifiable solutions** - Many work condition issues meet this criteria, particularly issues that have a history of being contentious with employees based on unpopular management action. Simple issues are typically responded to by management, so the ones that remain are normally the more complex with more difficult solutions.

- **Problem where team members' areas of expertise could help identify solutions** – Depending on the particular work condition issue, the team members are perhaps in the best position to identify potential solutions to problems and how they would impact the operation.
- **Problem with limited or identifiable timelines** – Work condition projects are perhaps the best example of problems with limited timelines, or where a "finish line" is easily identified.
- **Issue where scientific analysis and measurement is possible** – Measurement and analysis of work condition problems are often readily available. Many have been analyzed before (as we shall see, financial constraints after analysis are often the most important obstacle to resolving these issues).
- **Direct impact on internal and external customers** – These issues directly impact internal customers – the employees who are required to deal with the unsatisfactory work condition. These conditions may also reduce productivity or quality, having a direct impact on external customers as well.
- **Meaningful to employees** – By their very nature, work condition issues are usually the most meaningful to employees.
- **Cuts across departments** – Work condition issues are very likely to impact more than one department.
- **Not a process in transition** – Sometimes work condition problems are a result of transitional issues in companies. Those issues are less resolvable in a team-oriented situation. In order to meet this criteria, managers must identify problems that are not transitory.

The advantages to choosing work condition projects for team processes are similar to those of safety projects. They both tend to express compassion for employees and are typically very popular causes. Both issues directly impact the day-to-day working life of employees.

The disadvantage to most work condition programs is that they can be expensive. Most employers do not allow poor working conditions as a rule. Therefore, where poor work conditions are not due to simple laziness or poor management, they are usually a result of limited resources or expense.

Expense is a very important aspect to the process of identifying whether an employee involvement initiative should be used on a work condition issue. If management is not prepared to respond to the work condition or to expend resources on solving it, it should never be chosen as a team topic.

One of the best approaches to resolving these issues is to identify budgetary constraints and to allow the team to work within those constraints. These guidelines force employees to make business decisions just like managers. The positive result of using this approach is that employees are encouraged to use creativity in solving the problem and/or they gain increased appreciation for the resource issues facing managers.

Client Story: Work Conditions Teams in Action

A manufacturing client of ours fabricates wood and metal products. We surveyed the company, and it received relatively typical scores. Work conditions rated very low, next to advancement and pay and benefits issues. However, the client was in a very competitive industry and regularly conducted wage and benefit surveys to ensure the company was competitive in this area. Therefore, we determined that frustrations exhibited regarding wages would need to be attacked from an employee communications standpoint and not through the expenditure of additional resources.

We identified the work conditions issue as a potential win-win for the company. Focus group sessions were conducted in conjunction with communicating survey results to identify the work condition problems in the plant. It became evident during the course of those meetings that the biggest complaint was over the amount of dust in the air.

Some employees treated this as a safety issue, but most simply complained of the fact that it was hot and sometimes uncomfortable to breathe. A few months earlier, the employer had a safety analysis performed at the plant to ensure that there was not a breathing hazard. There was not. Nevertheless, employees still complained about the work condition, and some still viewed the workplace unsafe.

Upon identifying this issue in focus groups, we went back to the company's top management and explained that this met our criteria of an effective subject for team-oriented problem solving. The employer noted that this issue had been examined several times before and any potential solution was just too expensive to implement.

This impasse existed before the union organizing campaign and had to be overcome in order to make any move to improve the dusty work condition frustrations among the employees in the plant. After discussing the possible options for dealing with the problem, we suggested that the employer think about if there was any money that could be budgeted to solve the problem. After some debate, a modest budget was established to work on the problem.

Once the budget was established, we asked for a team of employees, including an engineer and several employees from both the wood and metal departments, to work together. The difficult task was to come up with a solution to the ventilation problem within the identified budget.

Team members initially received training on facilitation of team meetings and on team-oriented problem solving. An outside facilitator from our company conducted the training. The facilitator explained budgetary parameters and helped the committee establish its mission statement, goals and timeline. After this, the only assistance from our company came in reviewing minutes from the meetings and suggesting ways to overcome roadblocks and obstacles. The onsite facilitator (an hourly employee from the company) handled the rest of the meetings.

The team met perhaps a half dozen times over the course of the next several weeks. The employees identified vendors of high-powered fans that they believed, if properly placed, would relieve the ventilation issues within the budgetary limitations. The team had two vendors bring in samples. During the course of this process, the vendors began to bid against each other. Ultimately the employees were able to secure a large fan and install it in the area where the majority of the dust was being created.

The same group of employees was surveyed approximately a year later. The overall score on working conditions improved over 12 percent, with

almost 70 percent of the employees responding favorably to statements regarding the work environment in the company.

Legal Issues

Like the use of employee opinion surveys, employers who use teams in an environment where union organizing has occurred recently must take extra care to understand the legal environment. The NLRB rules that govern the use of workplace teams apply equally to all organizations covered by the NLRA (even those who have experienced no union organizing activity). Nevertheless, it is realistically those companies who have been through organizing activity (and whose activities are therefore being closely monitored by unions) who will need to pay closest attention to the rules that follow.

Section 8(a)(2) of the NLRA prohibits employers from dominating or supporting any group of employees that falls under the broad definition of a "labor organization" in section 2(5) of the Act.[32] In several cases the NLRB has found that teams or committees of employees constitute "labor organizations" and, due to the fact that they are supported or under the control of the company, are unlawful under section 8(a)(2).[33]

The prohibition of 8(a)(2) was originally intended to prevent "company unions," a common response by employers in the first half of the 20th century to avoid a true "arms length" bargaining relationship with an

---

[32] Section 2(5) defines a "labor organization" as an entity that "exists for the purpose, in whole or in part, of *dealing with* employers concerning grievances, labor disputes, wages, rates of pay, hours of employment, or conditions of work." (Emphasis added.)

[33] *See e.g. Electromation, Inc.*, 309 NLRB 990 (1992), enfd. 35 F.3d 1148 (7th Cir. 1994); *E.I du Pont & Co.* 311 NLRB 893 (1993); *Keeler Brass Co.*, 317 NLRB 1110 (1995).

independent union.[34] In the years since section 8(a)(2) was enacted, particularly in the last two decades with the increased use of more decentralized and empowered work teams in the workplace, the NLRB and the courts have struggled with distinguishing between cooperation (which the courts allow) and domination (which is prohibited by the Act).[35]

This struggle to distinguish between cooperation and domination turns on the NLRB's interpretation of "dealing with." The NLRB described its formulation recently in its decision in *Crown Cork & Seal Company,* 334 NLRB No. 92 (2001):

> One of the required elements for "labor organization" status under Section 2(5) is that the entity "exists for the purpose, in whole or in part, of *dealing with* employers concerning grievances, labor disputes, wages, rates of pay, hours of employment, or conditions of work." (Emphasis added.) The Board explained that "dealing with" contemplates "a bilateral mechanism involving proposals from the employee committee concerning the subjects listed in Section 2(5), coupled with real or apparent consideration of those proposals by management." *Electromation, Inc.,* 309 NLRB 990, 995 fn. 21 (1992) enfd. 35 F.3d 1148 (7th Cir. 1994). "That 'bilateral mechanism' ordinarily entails a pattern or practiced in which a group of employees, over time, makes proposals to management, [and] management responds to these proposals by acceptance or rejection by word or deed. ..." *E.I. du Pont & Co.,* 311 NLRB 893, 894 (1993).[36]

Not all employee committees or work teams are "labor organizations" subject to the restrictions of 8(a)(2).

---

[34] *See* Hardin, et al. (eds.), *The Developing Labor Law,* 3rd edition (BNA Books 1996), pp. 298-299.

[35] *See Id.,* pp. 299-300.

[36] *Compare General Foods Corp.,* 231 NLRB 1232 (1977) (job enrichment program delegating responsibility to employees normally assigned to management not "dealing with" under Section 2(5)).

In *Crown Cork & Seal Company,* 334 NLRB No. 92 (2001), the NLRB recently outlined the factors it considers when determining whether an employee committee is "labor organization" under section 2(5) of the Act.

In *Crown Cork & Seal Company* the company had seven committees examined by the Board. They were part of the "Socio-Tech System" that was designed to delegate to employees substantial authority to operate the plant. The seven committees in question included combinations of management, production and maintenance employees. Four of the committees were production teams – every employee in the plant participated on one of these four teams. The remaining three committees were the Organizational Review Board (ORB), the Advancement Certification Board (ACB) and the Safety Committee. Many of the decisions of these committees were reviewed by the management team *Crown Cork & Seal Company,* 334 NLRB No. 92 (2001).

The ORB monitored plant policies to ensure they are administered fairly and consistently by each of the plant production teams. The ORB regularly recommended changes to the plant manager or management team in policies, hours, layoffs, smoking rules, vacations and other terms and conditions of employment. The ORB also reviewed recommendations by the production team to terminate, suspend or discipline an employee. The plant manager testified that he rarely, if ever, rejected a recommendation of the ORB. *Crown Cork & Seal Company,* 334 NLRB No. 92 (2001).

The committees were not allowed to operate outside of established parameters. One example identified was when the ORB recommended a layoff procedure with a provision for seniority. The management team returned the recommendation to the ORB with a note that "we do not have seniority in this plant" and the final version did not include seniority as a factor. *Crown Cork & Seal Company,* 334 NLRB No. 92 (2001).

The ACB, which administered a pay for skills program in the plant, certified skill levels of employees and recommended them for raises. The Safety Committee reviewed any accidents in the plant and would make recommendations to help make the plant safe. The plant manager never overruled a recommendation of either the ACB or the Safety Committee. *Crown Cork & Seal Company,* 334 NLRB No. 92 (2001).

The NLRB found that the Socio Tech System, like the job enrichment program in *General Foods,* was a flat delegation of management authority to production employees. The Board found that the power exercised by the committees was "managerial." However, the Board held that the committees do not "deal with" management but instead they "perform essentially management functions." *Crown Cork & Seal Company,* 334 NLRB No. 92 (2001).

The Board rejected the argument that the act of making recommendations to the plant manager that could be rejected by him is in effect "dealing with" management. The Board distinguished the act of sending recommendations between levels of authority from the exchange of proposals in a bargaining context. The Board compared the sending up of recommendations by the committee to be very much like the sending up of a recommendation by a supervisory employee in a more traditional plant. The Board felt that the Socio Tech committees simply played the same role as a supervisor in the traditional plant. "[T]he seven committees *are* management," in their respective areas of authority, the Board held. *Crown Cork & Seal Company*, 334 NLRB No. 92 (2001) (Emphasis in original).

Therefore, an employer wishing to avoid difficulty under Section 8(a)(2) should take great care to ensure that any employee committee or team is given broad discretion to act within its area of authority. The factors considered most important in *Crown Cork & Seal* were:

- The number of times a committee recommendation was rejected by higher levels of management
- The weight given to committee recommendations (when faced with contrary recommendations from other managers)
- The types of tasks delegated to the committee (typically "managerial" tasks)
- Whether there appears to be any "back and forth" between the committee and management (versus simply forcing committee to act within its area of authority)

Obviously these cases are very fact-intensive, and there is no way to be certain that any committee or team will satisfy the NLRB requirements. This fact often frustrates employers (I guess the Board wonders why should this issue be any more certain than the remainder of labor law). As frustrating as the law might be, this should not diminish in any way the incentive to use teams where they can be effective. The key is to clearly identify the parameters for the team and then give them substantial authority to act within those parameters.

Conclusion

Teams are not for everyone. Employee involvement takes effort and commitment on the part of both management and employees. This work of team problem-solving is above and beyond the normal day-to-day activities of employees. Some employees are motivated to participate; others are not. As we have discussed, some projects are well suited for this approach while others are not. However, if management is capable of identifying projects suitable for teams and can identify groups of employees who will do an effective job in a team environment, the programs can be highly successful.

Ultimately, employees who participate in employee involvement programs feel they are more connected with the company. These employees make a real contribution and have control over their work environment. Our experience is that effective implementation of team-based approaches when solving problems results not only in increased satisfaction over contentious issues, but also increased credibility of supervision and top management. Most importantly, it increases employee satisfaction with their jobs.

Chapter 9

Recruiting, Hiring and Pre-Employment Screening

*"You can't be all things to all people.
But I can be all things to the people I select."*
Donald Neuenschwande

What You'll Learn In This Chapter
- How selection techniques can transform your employee relations environment
- Why an effective hiring program is the first step to employee retention
- The disadvantages of relying on "historical" data when hiring instead of present evidence of competency
- Strategies for creating narrow, objectively observable interviewing criteria
- The five keys to conducting a good interview
- Whether job simulations can improve your selection process and hints on recruiting

Employers today settle for less and less when it comes to hiring. These employers end up hiring anyone who walks through the door. That, my friends, is a recipe for trouble.

You've heard this (or maybe even said it) before: "I knew that guy was trouble the minute I hired him. I bent over backwards to give him a chance to work out, and the thanks I get is an NLRB petition! How could I be so stupid?"

Of course there are those *"high standards"* folks with big impact interviewing techniques like:

> "What's your name?"
> "Joe."
> "Ever been in a union, Joe?"
> "Yeah, I was in one back in the 70s when I was bagging groceries for my local supermarket. High school job."
> "Well, Joe, let me tell you how things run around here. We don't have a union here and we don't need your kind coming in here with your bright ideas trying to change that. You know Joe, I didn't like your look from the start. I think maybe you better just look for work somewhere else."

While these people make good clients for labor lawyers, they make even worse hiring decisions than companies that don't interview at all.

Employers should not be concerned with prior union membership[37]; instead they should focus on hiring people who are self-directed, team-oriented, committed to their work quality and open to coaching from co-workers and supervisors. Research indicates that self-directed and independent-minded people with a strong sense of commitment to the quality of

---

[37] This should go without saying, but in addition to being a poor hiring practice, it is a violation of Section 8(a)(3) of the National Labor Relations Act to select people based on their prior union membership, their suspected union sympathy or even the fact that they are known to be professional organizers seeking employment solely to organize the employer. *See e.g. Phelps Dodge Corp. v. NLRB*, 313 U.S. 177 (1941) (union members); *NLRB v. Electrical Workers Local 322 (Bechtel Power Corp.)*, 597 F.2d 1326 (10th Cir. 1979) (non-members); *NLRB v. Town & Country Electric*, 516 U.S. 85 (1995) (paid union organizers). For more information on this or other labor law questions, talk to your labor counsel and *see* Hardin, et al. eds, *The Developing Labor Law*, (BNA Books, 1996 and supplements).

their work performance are typically less likely to vote for a union[38] (again, I stress that this is not a reason for adopting such a program, but it is a potential side-effect of focusing your hiring in this area). These individuals are also more likely to be involved in community activities, prefer pay-for-performance arrangements and are normally high performers in their jobs. Are you beginning to see any trends here?

Community and Work Involvement: Union Prevention Tools?

Studies by scholars friendly with organized labor suggest that community involvement of workers significantly reduces their likelihood of being involved with a union. One such study concludes:

"To summarize, the effect of community involvement, net of the effects of standard model predictors, is to lower the likelihood of voting pro-union in a certification election. The findings suggest that community involvement effectively competes with unionization for individual allegiances. In addition to the influence of employment and workplace issues on respondents' desires to unionize, involvement in community organizations tends to reduce the desire of respondents to unionize their workplaces."[39]

These studies also suggest that worker involvement in Employee Involvement Programs (EIP's) significantly

---

[38] For many examples, *see* Brofenbrenner et al., eds., *Organizing to Win: New Research on Union Strategies* (Cornell University Press, 1998); the best explicit discussion of the issue from a hiring policy standpoint I have ever read is in Saltzman, "Job Applicant Screening By A Japanese Transplant: A Union-Avoidance Tactic," 49 *Industrial and Labor Relations Review* 88-104 (1995).
[39] Cornfield, McCammon, McDaniel and Eatman, "In the Community or In the Union?" *Organizing to Win: New Research on Union Strategies* (Cornell University Press, 1998), p. 255.

reduces the likelihood employees will turn to unions. Another study concludes:

"The difference in the union win rates between campaigns in which employee-involvement programs existed and those in which they did not is striking: the union won in 48 percent of all the elections when there were no EIP's but in only 30 percent of all the elections when there were EIP's."[40]

The following table summarizes some more of this research.[41] This study suggests that employee involvement in community organizations or churches can reduce the likelihood of support for unionization by over 15%. This table describes the percentage increase or decrease in the odds of voting pro-union in a certification election for respondents with specific characteristics compared with those without such characteristics.

Characteristic	Increase/Decrease In Odds (in Percent)
Has high job autonomy (versus moderately high autonomy)	-9.7%
Perceives that employer gives raises for performance (versus respondent who does not have such perception)	-22.0%
Agrees that unions have too little power (versus indifferent respondent)	54.7%
Disagrees that unions hinder economic progress (versus indifferent respondent)	132.3%

---

[40] James Rundle, "Winning Hearts and Minds in the Era of Employee Involvement Programs," *Organizing to Win: New Research on Union Strategies* (Cornell University Press, 1998), p. 218.

[41] *See* Cornfield, McCammon, McDaniel and Eatman, *supra* note 39.

Black (versus white)	37.7%
5-9 years' work experience (versus <5 years)	-1.9%
Has two organizational memberships (versus one membership)	-18.2%
Attends religious services monthly (versus several times a year)	-15.0%

Unsophisticated, uneducated or simply unscrupulous employers often try to discern union sympathy during the interview process. One interviewing option is to ask people about whether they are prone to vote for a union or not. Of course this question is illegal. The other option is to try to hire independent, self-directed individuals committed to their work, without reference to (and without caring about) union sympathy. Not only is this legal, it is just smart business.

Take this opportunity to improve your employment selection process. Start asking the right questions – look for people who value on-the-job autonomy, want to be paid for high quality performance, are interested in employee involvement and appear to be committed to their employers. Look for people who are involved in community organizations. Stop worrying so much about whether someone has been a union member and start worrying about what kind of a performer they'll be. The good news is that this practice will not only keep you out of court, but is better for business and is the best predictor of whether someone will be a good performer and a valuable contributor to your organization.

Hiring for Results
One of the best places to start an employee retention program is in the hiring process. This seems counter-

intuitive to some, but the evidence is overwhelming – companies that do a good job of hiring have fewer problems with turnover and enjoy the benefit of a generally happier workforce.

Companies that hire anybody who walks in the door usually have turnover problems. They also tend to experience lower employee morale among the employees who do stay. By hiring individuals without a thorough selection process, you are more likely to employ someone who is either unskilled or otherwise unable to perform the job satisfactorily.

If the prospective employee does not have an accurate picture of what his job duties will be or is not screened sufficiently to ensure a proper fit into your work environment, the likelihood is that he will not remain an employee for very long. His leaving may be through self-ejection, i.e. quitting because the job wasn't what he thought it to be, or because the work was too difficult. His tenure may also end by termination due to his inability to perform the job properly.

Additionally, employees who have been with the company awhile are unlikely to accept a procession of new hires with open arms. They are often frustrated by this "revolving door" of new hires who (due to the poor screening process) are unable to do the work. This frustration will manifest itself in many ways. New employees will not be welcomed. (Why attach yourself to someone who won't be there in 90 days anyway?) Management will constantly be blamed for production problems because people are consistently hired who are unable to do the job. Thus, negativity permeates the workforce – new hires and longer-term employees are equally frustrated and unhappy.

Therefore, ineffective hiring practices perpetuate the problems of constant turnover and poor morale – it is a vicious cycle. So how does one go about creating a hiring process that can put the brakes on this treadmill? The solution is really not that complicated. It does, however, require a little work up front and consistent attention to the hiring process. Perhaps the most important point relevant to this issue is to develop a process and stick with it in every hiring decision. What follows is a description of how we assist companies in developing a hiring process.

The focus of the hiring process should be on competencies and not on history. The fact that someone has done a job in the past is certainly worth knowing. What is much more valuable is to know how they performed that job and, even more important, how they will do the job in the future. This information is rarely discovered when reviewing historical data on a job application or a resume'. It is something that must be demonstrated either during the interview or, better yet, by conducting a simulation. A process should be in place to evaluate not only "hard" skills but also "soft" skills that are necessary to effectively perform the job.

The place to start when developing a list of competencies necessary to job performance is to look at your high performing employees. Begin with a list of jobs for which you hire regularly. Underneath that list, make a list of high performing employees currently working in each of those jobs. Underneath that list of names should be a listing of specific competencies or job performance characteristics that make those individuals high performers. For example, look at their attendance, willingness to help others, professionalism, work quantity and quality, or other characteristics that make those employees high performers. These factors may be different for each job, but there will be many crossovers within the organization. It is very important that this list include objective, readily identifiable characteristics.

The table below lists some factors generally used in hiring. The first column describes the factors in language that is too broad, while the second column outlines narrower, more objective factors. Again, it is important to understand that the specific competencies required by a particular job will differ across job categories and companies. The key is to specifically identify the performance characteristics of high performing employees.

Broader **Less Objective Factors**	*Narrower* **More Objective Factors**
Good Attitude	• Willingness to make changes based on work demands • Willingness to pitch in on projects not technically part of employee's everyday job • Ability to influence co-workers to jointly solve problems
Good Attendance	• Almost always at work/meetings promptly and on schedule
Communication Skills	• Clear communicator in written and spoken form; able to understand verbal and written instructions
Organized	• Identifies most efficient or convenient order when accomplishing assigned tasks

Another important part of this exercise is to list objectively identifiable characteristics that are evident in poor performers. Therefore, a second list should be generated identifying poor performing employees and the objective considerations and characteristics of their performance.

This project can be very valuable when conducted in group sessions with supervisors or managers in charge of supervising the particular jobs in question. If these same supervisors or managers are making hiring decisions on those jobs, the information gathering process gains even greater importance – it can greatly improve the interviewing and selection skills of the hiring supervisors.

Once competencies are identified, the next step is to identify the interview questions that will elicit the appropriate information from a prospective employee. Questions must be carefully crafted to identify whether candidates have the high performance characteristics or not.

Once again, these questions should elicit objective information from the prospective employee regarding the competencies that you have identified with high performers. The questions should be reviewed by labor counsel to ensure that they are considered lawful under the myriad laws in place regarding discrimination and employment.

The table below includes some sample questions in various competencies.

Competency Area	Interview Questions
Initiative	• What ideas have you sold to management in the past? Why? • What happened? • How much information do you need to get started on an assignment?
Participative Culture	• Tell me about a team you were on. • What was the biggest success of your team? • What was the biggest challenge your team faced? • What characteristics make it hard for someone to work on a team?

	•	What do you find challenging about working on a team?
Interpersonal Skills	•	Give me an example of a co-worker, manager, or customer whom you find most difficult to communicate with. Why?
	•	What would you do if a co-worker made a derogatory comment about another co-worker?
Creativity Innovativeness	•	Describe a great idea that you have seen in your job recently.
	•	Why was it unique?
	•	Give an example of a situation at your previous employer when others knew more than you. How did you close the gap?

It is good practice to brainstorm a long list of possible questions and then have a group identify and evaluate the best ones. The next step in the process is to create a form that will provide consistency to the interview process. Once the interview form is developed, it should be used in all interviews. Each potential candidate for a job should be asked the same questions in the same environment. The idea is to create, as closely as possible, identical circumstances for the interviewing process. In this way candidates can be evaluated against each other more accurately.

There are a few golden rules of interviewing that should always be observed:
• Conduct interviews in a location that is private and free from interruptions.
• Make sure that you have fully prepared a consistent and objective interviewing process before seeing the first candidate.
• Enlist at least two individuals to separately interview all finalists for the job. This helps to reduce subjectivity.
• Rely on open-ended questions versus closed-ended or "yes" or "no" questions. Give the candidates an opportunity to respond fully using specific

examples from their lives. Insist that candidates answer all questions. Even if this causes uncomfortable silence sometimes, wait for them to answer the question. If a candidate gives an answer that is not specific enough or skirts around a question, repeat the question. Part of the interviewing process is to get comparable and objective answers to the questions.

- Take notes during the interview period and accurately write down the candidate's responses to the questions you have asked so that you can accurately compare responses at a later time.

These are some of the basics for conducting a good interview. There are, of course, a number of excellent texts and training courses available to help hone interviewing skills.

Pre-Employment Screening and Job Simulations

Many organizations today use pre-employment tests and job simulations as an important part of their hiring process. Again, the use of these tools is important to create a consistent and objective hiring environment where candidates can be compared rather than the "gut feeling" approach used by companies with a poor hiring record.

The decision on what screening tools to use depends primarily on the job for which you are hiring. A number of pre-employment screening tools are available on the market today. These range from competency-based computer software tests to high-end psychological profiles. The types of tests used in hiring for a particular position will depend primarily on the competencies required to perform the job. Entry level manufacturing positions probably do not require high level psychological testing. Requiring a candidate for the CEO position to take a typing test is likewise an ineffective use of screening time.

An increasing body of literature suggests the importance of emotional intelligence skills in our knowledge-based economy. I am convinced that the conclusions reached by these authors, if anything, understate the importance of soft skills in today's work environment. The ability to work together to solve complex business problems increasingly sets high performing companies apart from their less successful competitors. Today, perhaps more than ever, it is critically important to hire people with high emotional intelligence or "soft skills" and put into place systems that allow them to learn the technical or "hard skills" necessary for job performance once they are hired.

Many companies have turned to soft skills profiling of employees as a way to make better hiring decisions. A word of caution, however, about using any pre-employment test. In today's highly litigious environment, it is obviously very important that any pre-employment test pass the scrutiny of discrimination laws. Before using a test, it is always a good idea to talk to both the vendor and your labor counsel about the validity and appropriate use of pre-employment screening tools.

At risk of oversimplifying the issue, the bottom line is that the employer must be able to prove that any test administered is job-related and predictive (i.e. that the test accurately predicts existence of the job-related skills for which it tests). Once the test is proven job-related and predictive, it is also a good idea to periodically review the impact of that test on various classifications of workers, i.e., minorities, gender and age. If a testing tool appears to have an adverse impact on any protected classification, you should alert labor counsel immediately and review whether or not use of the test should continue.

Job simulation is another very productive screening tool. Whether we like to admit it or not, often people overstate their qualifications and skills on job applications and resumés. Job simulation is a way to identify skill levels of candidates by performing actual job tasks they will be required to perform every day. Another advantage of job simulation is that it provides a good preview of the job to prospective employees. This allows employees to decide, prior to accepting a job, whether the tasks required by that job are ones they want to perform on a daily basis. Many companies find that this preview further reduces turnover in the workforce.

Clearly, some positions are better suited for performance simulation than others. For instance, simulating a receptionist or assembly line job is significantly easier than simulating the duties of a CEO. Often companies will pick parts of a job to simulate in order to make administration simpler and repeatable. Again, the concerns related to job simulation are similar to those for other types of employment tests. The simulations should be objective and as similar as possible for each of the candidate tested. There should be an objective way to identify a "passing" or "failing" score or performance on the simulation. This test should be used as part of an overall hiring scheme, not the only factor.

Recruiting
Employers often complain when talking about tightening standards in the hiring process about the problem of just getting bodies in the door. These organizations do not understand the relationship

between poor selection procedures and high turnover. High turnover obviously creates greater pressure on the recruiting process – more bodies must get in the door to fill the spots left by former employees. However, great companies that do an excellent job of hiring have significantly fewer problems with recruiting. This is due in part to the fact that there are fewer positions to fill. Nevertheless, candidates must be sourced, and recruiting is an important part of the hiring process.

The recruiting process is tough. Again, a systematic approach is best. An important characteristic of effective recruiting processes is creativity. Many employers still source exclusively by running newspaper ads when they have job openings. However, high performing employers have learned that recruiting is an ongoing process, and if you wait until you have an opening before recruiting for that opening, you are likely to have continuing difficulty with filling positions.

The recruiting process should be approached in the same manner as identifying competencies in the hiring process. For example, look at high performing employees and identify how those individuals were sourced to your company. In this way you identify a broad list of recruiting sources – often much broader than people applying off the street or responding to newspaper ads. In addition to this list, think of other innovative recruiting methods. Companies today use many resources, including their web sites, open house receptions, job fairs, radio and cable television ads, and many other sources. An almost limitless number of opportunities exist for finding potential candidates. Employers also are learning that by reaching out to minority and non-traditional communities (disabled, retirees, etc.) they are able to source more and more talent into their organization.

As alluded to earlier, implementing a consistent recruiting process is vitally important. By networking and searching for talent on an ongoing basis, a company can ensure that it always has a qualified pool of applicants and potential employees. at all times will help in times when there is a shortage. As good candidates identify themselves, stay in touch with them, even if there are no jobs available at the time.

The recruiting, selection and hiring process is complicated and difficult. It is, nevertheless, one of the most important things a company must do in order to sustain its success and to grow. Decisions made about hiring are increasingly the most important decisions made by organizations. As we proceed further into a knowledge-based economy, this importance will only solidify. Companies that concentrate and invest time and energy on the hiring process will see great returns, not only in employee morale, but also on the bottom line.

They're Hired, Now What? Orientation Programs

"A vision is not a vision unless it says yes to some ideas and no to others, inspires people and is a reason to get out of bed in the morning and come to work."
Gifford Pinchot

What You'll Learn In This Chapter
- You never get a second chance to make a first impression – why the orientation process is critical
- Common mistakes made in the orientation process
- Strategies for planning new hire orientation
- Why you should consider lengthening the time of your new hire orientation
- How to involve co-workers in the new hire orientation process

One often-overlooked area for an employee relations program is the new hire orientation process. This area is overlooked due to the pressures involved in getting a new employee up to speed. Most employers do not begin the hiring process until there is an opening. Therefore, after the several weeks spent sourcing, recruiting, interviewing and then making a job offer to a candidate, it is imperative to get the individual to work as soon as possible. This is especially true in high turnover companies.

As with companies that do a poor job of hiring, companies that make little effort to orient new employees reinforce the cycle of turnover evident in many businesses today. There are several reasons for this. First, employees who begin working in an environment in which they are unsure of their responsibilities or where that job fits into the company, often become frustrated and anxious, which can lead to poor performance.

During this critical early period, such feelings can cause employees to self eject. ("That job just wasn't what I thought it would be".) Even worse, employees in this dilemma are often terminated for failure to make their "90-day probation." Discharge often occurs when supervisors determine a new employee is not up to speed. ("They just don't get it".) Companies with these problems are often failing to teach basic skills during the orientation process.

A second reason the orientation period is so critical is because the company has the full attention of the new hire. Newly hired employees are typically happy to land a job and, at this time perhaps more than any other, are willing to give the employer the benefit of the doubt on most employment issues. Therefore, it is critical during this period of good will to impart as much positive information as possible. This is also a good time to communicate potentially negative information or challenges that the employee may face during his or her employment. The employer has a captive audience and can explain its policies before the employee is biased from contact with negative employees.

This platform is particularly important in an environment with vulnerability to union organizing. For example, the company may want to take this opportunity to communicate reasons behind policies and procedures that are considered negative by a vocal minority of the work force. Examples of these include attendance policies, appeal processes for work disputes, and benefit or claim procedures. This time is also a good opportunity to communicate the company's union-free philosophy. While the purpose of the orientation process should be positive and not concentrate on lots of rules and regulations, it is an excellent opportunity to "choose your battles" and get the company's position on key issues in the forefront.

The orientation process is also one of the few opportunities a company has to communicate, with the full attention of the employee, important issues that build loyalty to the company. These issues include company history, discussion of the business environment and market in which the company competes and the company's philosophy.

Many companies communicate this information through an orientation video. A video can be sent home with employees so they, along with their families, can learn more about the company. This is a very effective tool when used to communicate general background information. Orientation videos are less well utilized to communicate information that might change on a frequent basis, like benefits and policy related issues.

Finally, the new hire orientation process should be fun and enjoyable for the employee. Many companies fall into one of two extremes in their orientation process. They might adopt a "trial by fire" approach, where the employee is dropped into his or her new position with the company with very little information, if any. Other companies go to the opposite extreme, trying to make their employees experts on every possible issue that they might face. These companies use a very rigid process, which may include testing on policies and procedures, signing tons of documentation, and generally an overload of information. Neither of these two approaches is much fun for the employee being oriented.

Instead of these extremes, a measured approach should be used that accomplishes both goals: acclimating employees to their new positions and communicating valuable information to the employees. The process should first and foremost be designed to give the employees a sense of belonging and make them confident in the decision they made to work for the company.

The labor market is not such that an employee will be happy just to have received a job. It is very important, even if there are a number of candidates for a position, to make sure that the one chosen feels good about his or her decision for the long term. If this effort is made consistently with every new hire, the company is setting itself up to succeed.

Undoubtedly, mistakes will be made in the hiring process, and some employees may end up becoming "bad eggs." However, by treating the orientation process as an opportunity to motivate and instill good feelings toward the company, there is much less likelihood of an employee automatically bad-mouthing the employer when given an opportunity.

In the long term, an effective orientation process will show results in increased employee morale and increased good will toward the company. Although every employer must be vigilant in ensuring that employee discontent over issues and concerns is dealt with effectively, there will be less likelihood that issues will snowball out of control in a work force that is positively inclined toward the employer from the beginning.

Common Mistakes

Think for a moment about your current orientation process and compare it to some of the common mistakes made by companies when orienting new employees. Some of these have been previewed earlier, but they will be listed here for ease of reference. The table below summarizes some of the most common mistakes:

Employees given a voluminous handbook or policy manual with little or no explanation.
Employees given a lengthy policy manual or handbook and extensive instructions over minor policies with which they will have little daily experience.
Employees immediately put on the job with little or no "low risk" preparation for performing the job.
Failure to give employees enough opportunity to meet co-workers and supervisors.
Spending an inordinate amount of time filling out forms and paperwork.
Including too much information in a short amount of time.
Failure to include social activities as part of the orientation process.
Failure to devote personalized attention during the orientation process.

Strategies to Improve the Employee Orientation Process

There are a number of strategies one can employ to improve and invigorate the orientation process. A few have been outlined earlier and many more can be surmised from the list of don'ts in the previous table. Here we will outline a few of the more creative ideas for improving the orientation process.

Plan the Orientation Process

Make sure that planning the orientation process is done with the goal of making it as interesting and enjoyable for the participant as possible. First impressions are most important, so it is critical to have the first morning well planned. Activities could include a reception for the new employee hosted by the employee's supervisor and work group.

Avoid beginning the first day of orientation by forcing the new employee to fill out a lot of forms. If this must be part of the orientation process, save it for later, toward the middle of the day. Structure each day of orientation around a core group of ideas or a particular area of training. Establish an agenda and a set of goals for each day and communicate that to the employee. Most important, include as many pleasant and enjoyable activities as possible during the orientation period.

Lessons From Orienting Executives

Several cutting-edge businesses have recently incorporated innovative orientation strategies in their new-hire process for executives. These techniques offer some insight into potential orientation techniques for all positions in an organization.

Jack in the Box, the fast-food chain, requires its new regional vice presidents to spend a month working in the restaurants they will ultimately manage. This includes everything from mopping floors to flipping burgers. These managers will have a better understanding of the day-to-day pressures faced by the people reporting to them and have a clearer understanding of the business environment than those who have never worked in a fast-food store.

Yet that is not the end of the orientation process for Jack in the Box executives. For another month, they shadow other executives and develop a personal strategic plan for their first year in their new position.

The results? Retention among executives who have gone through the program is much higher than in comparable businesses.

The Limited, a clothing retailer, has a program called "on-boarding" for its new executives. These employees spend a month with no responsibility for the job tasks on which they will spend the rest of their career. Instead they spend the month selling clothes, investigating competitors and learning about the company's history and future plans. Even after the first month, these executives only gain responsibility for their new positions part time during the ensuing several months. The idea, once again, is to ensure that executives thoroughly understand the company, its philosophy and its people.

While giving new hires a month or two to learn about the business may seem a little extreme, these examples show the importance that some companies place on the orientation process. Knowing your day-to-day job tasks is important. Understanding how your job fits into the business and knowing the responsibilities of others can help individuals at all levels. It sets up workers for long-term employment. They feel like they are part of a team or family. This should be the goal for any orientation program.

Include Co-Workers and Supervisors in the Orientation Process

This makes it more interesting for the new employee and also makes the orientation process more inclusive in the company. It creates buy-in from the rest of the employees. The more people involved, the more exciting it will be. Including employees in the process also creates an opportunity to empower co-workers. If employees are involved in orienting new employees, their feeling about the value of the orientation program increases dramatically. Employee involvement also creates additional opportunities for interactions between co-workers and supervisors.

Even though involving employees in the orientation process can create strains, particularly during periods where the workload is high, the effort is worthwhile. Time to get acquainted must be allocated for co-workers and the new employee. This time should be in addition to actual on-the-job training. If possible, job training should occur first in a classroom setting or some other environment where there is little risk (i.e. a simulated operating station designed for training purposes) so that the new employee can practice without worrying about messing up job production.

Increase the Length of Time

Don't try to hurry the orientation schedule by compressing the allotted time. This does not mean that orientation must last a week or more, although some jobs require an extensive amount of training. The time should be sufficient to thoroughly acclimate the new employee. Throwing an employee handbook to new employees, then sending them out on the line for their first day is unacceptable.

The key aim for orientation should be to acclimate new employees to their jobs and the company in a measured fashion. Most orientation programs should last a minimum of two days and should include sessions on:
- Company history
- Business issues and market considerations
- Overview of the various departments of the organization and how they fit together
- Tour of the facility

- Overview of important company policies and benefits
- Filling out the necessary paperwork and forms
- Skills training
- Safety training
- At least one social event (welcome reception, lunch with supervisor, welcoming party, etc.)

Depending upon the complexity of the job, the orientation process may last a week or longer. The bulk of the additional time may be spent in skills training with some on-the-job training as a follow-up.

All orientation programs should be designed to include some sort of regular follow-up during the orientation or probationary period. Again, this practice creates a habit of communicating performance expectations and development with employees, which hopefully will carry on beyond the orientation period. These sessions can be conducted alternately between a human resources representative and the immediate supervisor.

There is an old cliché that you never get a second chance to make a first impression. This is exactly the way companies should approach the orientation process. Getting employees started on the right foot helps to create a stream of positively motivated workers ready to work, knowledgeable about the goals and rules of the company. These employees will be better prepared to defend the company if they understand the motivation behind rules, procedures and business practices. Well-oriented employees are also more productive. Finally, including co-workers in the orientation process improves teamwork and maximizes opportunities for empowering highly effective hourly employees. As the saying goes, if you miss this opportunity, you never get it back.

Chapter 11

Recognition and Motivation Strategies

"What every genuine philosopher (every genuine man, in fact) craves most is praise—although the philosophers generally call it 'recognition'."
William James

What You'll Learn In This Chapter
- ❑ That recognition, and not money, is the number one motivator of employees
- ❑ Why recognition and motivation is so difficult for most companies
- ❑ Low and no cost motivation programs
- ❑ Informal and formal recognition strategies
- ❑ Legal issues with implementing recognition or motivation programs

Survey after survey we conduct shows that money is <u>not</u> the biggest motivator of employees. Instead, the number one motivator for employees is receiving recognition for a job well done. While low pay or poor benefits are great ways to de-motivate workers, recognition is the route to high performance.

Recognition is much more difficult for a company to consistently deliver than changes in pay and benefit programs. Perhaps the fact that this quality is so seldom used explains why recognition for a job well done is such a highly motivating factor. Employee recognition at its best is personal and specific to the individual's performance of a particular task. There is no "off the shelf" program that makes this happen.

Only consistent effort and practice by managers, supervisors and ultimately co-workers is effective. Constant and verbal employee appreciation has to become part of your business philosophy.

A company can employ a number of strategies to improve its record in the areas of recognition and motivation. Ultimately any strategy employed must be consistent with the business environment and goals of the company. An impromptu trip to a movie theater, for example, probably will not motivate employees of a movie theater. The same reward may be highly motivating to employees of a retail store. Ultimately, a contrived recognition program will be seen for exactly what it is and may have a negative impact on employee motivation. Instead, companies should think of as many strategies as they can to give sincere acknowledgement, then adopt the ones that seem to fit best within their organization.

Bob Nelson, a nationally recognized expert on motivation strategies for employees, has written several books on motivating, rewarding and energizing employees.[42] He focuses on three important aspects of rewards that bear repeating. First, match the reward to the person. A program providing the exact same reward to all employees will be less motivating than one rewarding individual performance on an individual basis. The more personal the reward, the more motivating it will be.

Nelson believes the second component of a successful reward program is matching the reward to the achievement. In other words, significant achievements receive greater rewards than small

---

[42] *See 1001 Ways to Energize Employees,* (Workman Publishing, 1997) and *1001 Ways to Reward Employees,* (Workman Publishing, 1994).

achievements. This is not to say that small achievements should not be rewarded, however. Instead, achievements should be rewarded in proportion to their value to the company, the effort of the individual, or the degree of innovation required.

Nelson's third strategy is to be timely and specific. This means that you reward successful performance when it occurs and specifically identify what is being rewarded.

Another important consideration with any reward program is to "mix it up." No matter how great or how well conceived a reward program you develop, after a period of time it will be considered "part of the package" and no longer motivating. This is the irony of rewarding only through compensation. A $1,000 bonus in one year may be highly motivating. However, a $500 bonus the following year, while certainly a bonus, may be considered negatively in the context of prior rewards. For this reason, it is very important to mix up rewards and recognition programs using a variety of different methods consistent with business goals of the company.

As mentioned, the reason reward and motivation programs are so difficult to successfully implement is that they require a lot more attention than compensation-based programs. There are no shortcuts. Employers must know what their employees are doing at work, know what they are proud of outside of work, and know what they like and don't like. Lapses in the program will tend to de-motivate employees.

The programs also have to be stepped. An employee who is consistently performing a function that was rewarded and has now become a habit, no longer needs to be rewarded for performing that function, but should be rewarded for performing some additional function. In this sense, there will be a continuous improvement aspect to the reward program.

There are a variety of strategies, both no cost and low cost, that employers can use to inexpensively reward employees and increase employee motivation. It is beyond the scope of this book to list all the different methods available. I will highlight a few good options as well as resources for learning other motivation strategies. More important for our purposes is discussing implementation of these reward and motivation strategies as part of an overall employee relations program.

No Cost and Low Cost Motivation Strategies
An employer can utilize a number of little to no cost strategies to motivate employees. These can be both informal and formal. Every employer should take time and effort to identify the best options for their particular workforce. Sometimes it is a good idea to solicit employees' input in the process of identifying motivational rewards.

Start simply. Have lunch catered to celebrate an individual's recent accomplishment. Host an impromptu ice cream social. Make a plaque commemorating a great accomplishment. Give an employee a partial day with pay to donate to his or her favorite charity. Hold short meetings for the express purpose of commemorating a success. Ring a bell to signify a new sale or client.

Look for motivational opportunities in your "normal" daily routine. *Fast Company* magazine has an article each month called "Meeting I Never Miss," which has given me several ideas for motivational meetings. One issue recently discussed a meeting called "First Friday," held at a startup company in Atlanta. This meeting includes all 120 employees of the company and starts by welcoming new employees. New employees introduce themselves and explain why they joined the company – each is also given a standing ovation by their peers. Next, each department updates the company on their successes and projects. Each team decides on the format for its presentation – often teams will use skits to help educate the company on their projects. These sessions are highly motivational and provide plenty of opportunity for recognizing successes of individual team members.

Train your supervisors and managers on recognition strategies. As I mentioned earlier, one of the best resources I have found on the subject is a book by Bob Nelson titled *A Thousand and One Ways to Reward Employees*. He has written a companion book titled *A Thousand and One Ways to Energize Employees*. These two books are great references to use when developing motivation programs and I encourage your to get both of them when thinking about your program. Below is a list of just a few of the excellent ideas Nelson suggests for informal recognition rewards.

Informal Rewards

- Congratulate employees with personal notes or cards
- Give employees personal recognition – supervisor can have the president or the supervisor's manager call employees and thank them for a job well done
- Give employees a pat on the back or catch them doing something right
- Take out newspaper ads thanking employees by name
- Host a day of appreciation, office parties
- Purchase a trophy to pass around
- Present a personal gift related to the employee's hobby
- Make a batch of cookies for the employee
- Give tickets to an event, give movie passes, pay for a round of golf or give service gifts – free car wash, lawn service, etc.

- Give time off or cash

Formal Reward Programs

Formal rewards are obviously more structured than their informal counterparts. These rewards, while not always expensive, do tend to have more resources allocated to them. Since these are more formalized, more effort should be put into communicating the parameters of the program to ensure employees understand clearly any "rules" associated with earning the reward. While more trouble and expense than informal programs, a few of the ideas on this list (also suggestions from Nelson) can be highly motivating – the types of programs talked about for years. Suggestions include:

Formal Rewards

- Name an employee of the month (all stars, rookie of the year, etc.)
- Give performance "bucks" that can be redeemed for prizes or contests where winners get to participate in company advertising
- Implement employee suggestion programs where employees are rewarded a percentage of the savings their idea brings to the company or where there's a drawing for everyone who contributes a suggestion during a period of time
- Give stock options or "phantom stock options"
- Ask customers or guests to nominate or even reward employees based on good service
- Send a team on an outing (fishing, baseball game, golf, cruise or other vacation) after completion of a project
- Award perfect attendance bonus (cash, stock, drawing)
- Host quiz shows to promote knowledge of company information, a company-wide "Olympic" event
- Award tuition for college, match donations to an employee's college of choice or make a donation in the name of an employee to the charity of his or her choice
- Send employees to special seminars, workshops or meetings outside the company
- Allow high performing employees to make presentations to top managers on issues or to mentor during the orientation process
- Give time off to work for community service, political campaigns or to give blood

These lists are not intended to be exhaustive and are merely designed to suggest starting points for thinking about motivation and recognition programs.

Legal Issues

For businesses worried about third party intervention, the implementation and development of the motivation program in your company must be handled diligently and conscientiously. An employer is not allowed to promise or offer inducements to employees for the purpose of discouraging them from engaging in union organizing activity under Section 8(a)(1) of the NLRA.[43] The United States Supreme Court acknowledged in 1944 that employee free choice "may be induced by favors bestowed by the employer" and is therefore unlawful. *See Medo Photo Supply Corp. v. NLRB*, 321 US 678, 686 (1944).[44]

As with grants of pay and benefits, an employer is prohibited from offering an inducement to employees when either the timing or impact leads the Board to conclude that the employer's purpose is one of "impinging upon... freedom of choice for or against unionization, and is reasonably calculated to have that effect."[45] This includes not only pay increases, but also favorable changes to other aspects of the employment relationship.[46]

Companies should avoid any action or communication that in any way implies that a recognition or motivation program is in any way related to organizing activity. Take particular care to look at the

---

[43] *See* Hardin, et al. (eds.), *The Developing Labor Law, 3rd Edition* (BNA Books, 1996), pp. 115-119.
[44] For an in depth discussion of the legal issues surrounding the unlawful grant of pay or benefits changes, *see* Chapter 12 *infra*.
[45] *NLRB v. Exchange Parts Co.*, 375 US 405, 409 (1964).
[46] *See Id.* at 409 (employer announced changes in birthday holiday, and more favorable holiday and overtime scheduling before NLRB election).

timing of any such program. If recent union organizing activity has occurred in your company it is a good idea to have your labor counsel review any plans for implementing motivation or recognition programs in this environment.

Bear in mind a couple of additional strategies with respect to implementing a motivational program. First, the program should be public. All employees should be aware of the program and the standards should be well communicated. Second, the implementation of the program needs to be consistent and fair. Managers and supervisors must be encouraged to consistently recognize good performance within their work group.

Perhaps the best way to make sure managers are motivated is for top management to evaluate managers and supervisors based on how effectively they recognize and acknowledge excellence among their employees. A good plan is to tie part of the appraisal process (and even better, part of the compensation process) directly to implementation of these motivational strategies.

One could, for example, reward managers whose employees give the most suggestions in a suggestion program. You could track the number of formal and informal incidents of recognition that occurred under various programs that are implemented. The key factor in sustaining the program is to hold managers accountable for recognition and motivation of their employees.

If formalized programs are used where cash or other monetary incentives will be distributed, employees should have a say in the development of those programs. While they do not have to be involved in every motivation program, it is a good idea to have at least one program that is developed and preferably even managed by a group of employees. This group should have the authority to change the program and monitor its implementation.

Managing a program in this way has the dual advantages of relieving some of the pressure on management and ensuring that there are several alternative routes to recognition and motivation. Allowing employee participation also empowers employees, which we have seen is a critical aspect of union-free management.

Finally, the motivation and recognition program should be as varied as possible. As recognition and motivational programs become stale, they should be replaced. Depending on the various programs used, generally every six months to a year at least one of the motivational programs should be altered. This practice keeps the programs fresh and allows the company to tweak various motivational strategies and try out new ones.

Chapter 12

Show Me the Money – How to Deal Effectively With the Challenges of Pay and Benefits

"Money is better than poverty,
if only for financial reasons."
Woody Allen

What You'll Learn In This Chapter

- ❑ The paradox of pay and benefit frustrations
- ❑ How your exit interview process can identify key pay and benefit concerns
- ❑ Conducting a pay and benefit survey to attack external fairness issues
- ❑ Designing a pay and benefit plan to avoid internal fairness issues
- ❑ The disadvantages of keeping pay issues secret
- ❑ Legal issues regarding pay and benefit changes

Pay and benefits are common employee relations issues. Rarely do employees feel they are overpaid or even fairly compensated for their jobs. Virtually everyone longs for higher pay and better and cheaper benefits. Therefore, pay and benefits are issues that we are regularly called upon to deal with in at-risk companies. Given the observation just noted, employee frustration over pay and benefits is inevitable; creating total employee satisfaction on these issues is the "holy grail" that will never be attained.

The paradox of compensation and benefit frustration was perhaps best explained by Frederick Herzberg in his classic article on employee motivation in 1968.[47] In this article, Professor Herzberg explained his theory that wages and benefits (along with many other aspects of the employment relationship) are not considered motivators of employees. He likened these issues to "hygiene" factors, which is an apt metaphor.

Wages and benefits are, by and large, satisfiers of a basic need for most employees. It is assumed that employers will provide a fair wage and benefit package in exchange for the work performed. A pay and benefit system that does not meet this requirement is certainly a de-motivating factor for employees and often a key issue in a union organizing campaign. However, even the most generous wage and benefit package cannot prevent frustration leading to organizing campaigns in companies with poor employee relations practices.

Therefore, employers should focus their efforts on ensuring that wage and benefit packages (and administration of those packages) meet two factors: external and internal fairness. If these two qualities are met, the employer can expect to avoid the de-motivation resulting from poor or unfair wage and benefit packages and create opportunities that focus on other areas of employee motivation and company productivity.

External fairness refers to how the wage and benefit package compares to other companies. In other words, a company that pays wages or provides benefits less favorable than those of its competitors or

---

[47] "One More Time: How Do You Motivate Employees?" *Harvard Business Review*, January-February 1968.

others in its region will be perceived more negatively than other employers. Chances are that companies suffering under this perception will also experience high turnover if the area job market has any fluidity. This factor can be identified by reviewing turnover statistics and exit interviews.

Internal fairness refers to whether the system and procedures by which employees are paid or receive benefits are handled fairly within the company. This can relate to performance appraisal systems, merit increases, equal pay issues, the way raises are handled, decisions regarding who receives benefits, and the like. Each of these areas will be discussed separately.

Conducting Effective Exit Interviews

Many companies fail to take advantage of one of the best sources for identifying problems in their company – ex-employees. There are a number of excuses. Lack of time and the feeling that departing employees will not give honest feedback are two of the most frequently cited.

These objections are misguided. First, good companies do not have time to ignore input from departing employees. In today's fast-paced economy, companies must constantly seek to increase efficiency and productivity. Unfortunately many company cultures do not go out of their way to encourage feedback on these issues. Many employees are reluctant to offer suggestions on these issues, for fear that their managers may feel like they complain too often. Exiting employees are an excellent source of information about processes and procedures that are frustrating or can be improved.

Questions regarding the honesty of feedback are not without merit, but still do not make exit interviews worthless. It is vital to question the veracity of complaints during the exit interview process. Disgruntled employees (particularly those who have been terminated for cause) may have an ax to grind during the exit interview process. So, too, may employees who are afraid to "burn bridges" sugarcoat the problems they observed while working at the company. Nevertheless, these two groups of employees offer an interesting prism from which to view the company's problems.

Terminated employees may have anger toward their supervisor or manager, which should be considered when reviewing feedback from exit interviews. But these individuals also have the least amount to lose by complaining about the company. They often have good insights about the problems of the company, even if they are slanted a little to the negative. In addition, their complaints, if looked at in the context of many other exit interviews, can help management spot trends that are causing turnover.

Employees anxious to leave a good impression may try to put a positive spin on issues, but still will answer most questions truthfully. Once again, if their input is viewed as part of a trend of data it can be very valuable in identifying problem areas. Assurances of confidentiality can also help to get these individuals to open up during the exit interview process.

One method to help improve the data collected from exit interviews (and to reduce the likelihood that the circumstances surrounding an individual's exit will taint the data set) is to use an anonymous forced response exit interview questionnaire. This way all exit interviewees answer the same set of questions and the data collected, over time, can be analyzed as a larger sample. This reduces the likelihood that a single comment or incident will result in an overreaction while ensuring that the company receives accurate information about why employees leave the company.

Another valuable use of the exit interview tool is to assist in limiting legal liability often associated with ending the employment relationship. For example, many companies will ask questions about incidents of discrimination or workplace injury. If these issues are raised during the exit interview it gives the employer an opportunity to respond to potential lawsuits very early in the process, perhaps initiating dispute resolution techniques before a charge or lawsuit is even filed. Should the employee fail to identify issues of discrimination or workplace injury during the exit interview, then suddenly remember an incident after they leave the company (perhaps after running into their local plaintiffs' lawyer?) the exit interview form can become terrific evidence for the employer.

The exit interview is not a panacea, but it can provide valuable information for employer. For an example of an exit interview form, *see* Appendix 4.

External Fairness Issues

There are a number of issues an employer should examine when determining the external fairness of its pay and benefit program. First, the employer must have a consistent and clearly stated philosophy regarding pay standards. Is the goal to compensate employees at a level equal to similarly situated employees in:

- The top third of the industry?
- The mid-point of the industry?
- The mid-point of the local community?
- Or to pay a fair day's wage for a fair day's work?

Whatever the philosophy, it should be clearly stated and understood within the management group. Identify clear directives concerning what the philosophy entails from a management perspective. Once a philosophy has been stated, a program should be identified to help the company meet that stated goal. Therefore, if the company wants to pay in a certain range within its industry, regular wage and benefit surveys of other employers must be conducted. If the benchmark pay to meet is that of local competitors, then a survey should be conducted among that group. The key issue is to ensure that the employer implements a process of regularly accumulating information from which to benchmark wage and benefits practices.

What If We Can't Keep Up With Our Competitors?

Most employers do not pay below market rates because they want to. Often, business conditions require that labor costs be constrained, compelling employers to hold labor costs in line for extended periods of time. These circumstances are difficult for both employers and employees. Nevertheless, it is critical for employers to be up front with employees about the situation if they intend to retain their loyalty.

There is a huge difference in the minds of most people between someone who is being "cheap" and someone who is being frugal. Most employees understand when frugality is based on legitimate business factors that, if ignored, would detrimentally impact or possibly end the business. Employees may not necessarily like the situation, but when faced with the alternative of no job at all, most will help out.

Asking employees to forgo pay raises and work for less than market value to help the company cannot be a long-term strategy, but it can work during the tight

times. **In particular, if an employer has communicated its philosophy regarding wages and benefits effectively and its employees believe in the employer and trust in the philosophy, they are many times willing to make sacrifices for their company.** **This is particularly true where other "non-hygiene" factors are well handled in the company.**

In order to do an effective job of maintaining external fairness, an employer must regularly survey companies within its realm of comparison. Employers should regularly and as scientifically as possible, accumulate information regarding wages and benefits in the areas in which it intends to benchmark its packages. Employees regularly will approach a company, particularly when looking for a raise or improvement, with anecdotal evidence regarding the wages or benefits paid by other area companies. In order to effectively respond to this type of information, it is crucial for the employer to have both a well-stated philosophy regarding its wage and benefit practices as well as an identified series of data that it relies upon to formulate its wage and benefit practices.

Conducting an effective wage and benefit survey is a complicated process – a full description is beyond the scope of this text. Nevertheless, there are several key principles I will briefly outline here.

First, conduct the surveys at regular intervals. Certainly data more than a year or two old is no longer valid.

Second, the survey should be conducted in a scientific manner. Clearly identify the categories and identities of employers who fit into the benchmark group. There are a variety of sources from which to obtain data, including salary and benefit surveys conducted by consulting businesses, Chambers of Commerce, and industry groups. You may also choose to conduct your own survey. No matter what source the information comes from, there are a few critical points that must be adhered to in order to gather effective data:

- Make sure that job descriptions for the jobs being compared are explicit and reviewed carefully. Small differences in job descriptions or duties can make significant differences in the compensation required for the position.
- Include not only hourly rates but also bonuses, stock options, 401(k) programs, lump sum payments and the variety of other methods of compensation that are used in businesses today. Failing to account for these additional areas of compensation can skew estimates in survey comparisons.
- Make sure all elements of benefit programs are examined, including medical and dental networks, deductibles, co-pays, premium sharing arrangements, significant exclusions, out-of-pocket limits and the like.
- Ensure confidentiality of the information in order to obtain accurate, specific data. This can be accomplished by promising to share benefits without company names, or by asking an outside party to conduct the survey.

Once external data has been collected and compared, the employer has information to which it can compare its current pay rates with its stated philosophy on wage and benefits. If this comparison is unfavorable, then the system must be adjusted.

Internal Fairness

It is equally important to analyze the internal fairness of the compensation and benefit system. Internal fairness primarily examines the philosophy of the company with respect to how performance is evaluated and how the employer will ensure administration of wages and benefits is handled in a fair and non-discriminatory fashion. The first step in examining internal fairness, like external fairness, is identifying the company's philosophy. Philosophies can range from:

- Merit pay for performance
- Pay for longevity
- Across-the-board increases
- Gain sharing or profit sharing

Whatever the philosophy, it is important for a company to clearly state and follow its compensation philosophy.

Due to ethical, company liability and employee motivation concerns, it is critical to maintain internal compensation fairness. From a legal perspective, fairness in compensation is just a good business decision. The EEOC has initiated numerous equal pay claims to ensure that women and men doing similar work are paid the same. A number of class action lawsuits regarding wage and hour violations have resulted in large verdicts or settlements against employers who improperly administered pay policies. A number of other cases have been litigated where minorities have proven that pay practices were discriminatory. Lawsuits regarding these types of issues are incredibly expensive and can create a terrible public relations problem. Discriminatory pay practices are also just wrong.

In addition, unfairness or the perception of unfairness in pay policies can create huge employee morale problems that spill over into all other areas of the company. If employees believe that the compensation system is unfair, they automatically assume other policies are administered unfairly. Thus, they lose trust in top management and are de-motivated. This situation results in reduced productivity.

To avoid the issue, many employers try to keep wage and salary discussions completely under the table. Further, they severely discipline any employee who discusses wage and salary information and try very hard to keep this information top secret.[48] These employers are deceiving themselves. Your employees talk about money. There is no way to get around this fact.

Employees, through the grapevine, will discuss and (worse yet) speculate on all areas of wage and salary administration. The better job an employer does of hiding pay and salary information, the more likely it is that unreliable sources like the grapevine will be the only source. This often creates bigger problems and more misinformation. It is much better for the company to be up front regarding its compensation policies and administration. While this does not necessarily require that individuals know exactly what co-workers make, issues like pay ranges, particularly in the job categories immediately surrounding a particular employee, should be public knowledge.

Some pay systems tie salary increases to individual performance. By using performance appraisal scores

---

[48] The NLRB recently ruled (and the 6th Circuit enforced the decision) that a blanket policy prohibiting salary discussions among employees violates Section 8(a)(1) of the NLRA. *See NLRB v. Main Street Terrace Care Center*, 164 LRRM 2833 (6th Cir. 2000).

or some other measurement of performance, a merit-based pay system can be implemented that rewards employees making the greatest contribution to the profitability of the organization.

Many companies will add a component that stair-steps rewards within performance ranges based on that employee's current level of pay (i.e. lower paid employees are eligible for larger increases than higher paid employees within a particular salary range). This system can then scientifically place employees across varying performance levels into a particular rate increase zone. Although highly dependent on the performance rating capabilities of supervisors, the system is totally fair, easy to administer and financially sound.

Other systems base rewards on company performance, not individual performance. Gain-sharing and profit sharing are popular versions of this approach. These systems avoid the inherent difficulty in appraising individual performance (many companies feel that tying performance appraisals to pay decisions is very detrimental). They focus attention on company goals. When done properly, these programs are very good. The challenge is connecting employee performance to the larger company performance in a way that lets employees understand how their work impacts the bonus payout. If employees do not understand this connection the bonus payout is seen simply as an extra check and when company performance lags this creates a de-motivating situation (almost like announcing a wage freeze or cut).

Still other companies rely on across-the-board pay increases based entirely on wage survey information. These organizations either decide to keep things simple or wish to avoid the admittedly much more difficult pay programs that tie pay in some way to performance. There is nothing inherently wrong with such systems, they just do not take advantage of pay as a potential motivator for performance. However, if such a system is adopted to avoid discussions of individual or company performance this is a poor employee relations practice.

These are just a few examples of many that are available. The bottom line is that whatever system is decided upon should meet the external and internal fairness philosophies of the company and be well communicated to employees.

Legal Issues

A company involved in organizing activity must take extra caution when making changes to its pay and benefit system. As discussed in an earlier chapter, an employer is not allowed to promise or offer inducements to employees for the purpose of discouraging them from engaging in union organizing activity under Section 8(a)(1) of the NLRA.[49]

Changes in pay and benefit programs are among the most common tactics used by unscrupulous employers to sway the outcome of union elections in their favor.[50] The United States Supreme Court stated in 1944 that "[t]here could be no more obvious way of interfering with these rights of employees than by grants of wage increases upon the understanding that they would leave the union in return."[51] For this reason the NLRB presumes that giving benefits during an organizing campaign is objectionable unless the

---

[49] *See* Hardin, et al. (eds.), *The Developing Labor Law, 3rd Edition* (BNA Books, 1996), pp. 115-119.
[50] *See Medo Photo Supply Corp. v. NLRB*, 321 US 678, 686 (1944).
[51] *See Id.* at 686.

company can prove the timing was governed by factors other than the election.[52]

As discussed earlier, an employer is prohibited from offering an inducement to employees when either the timing or impact leads the Board to conclude that the employer's purpose is one of "impinging upon... freedom of choice for or against unionization, and is reasonably calculated to have that effect."[53]

The NLRB will examine a number of factors when determining whether the grant of a pay or benefit increase is unlawful. The Board will rule against an increase where it is: (1) given in the context of repeated references to the union; (2) made effective just before an election; (3) conforms to an earlier request by a union during the campaign; (4) announced before an election when it could reasonably be delayed until afterward; (5) otherwise announced in a way calculated to influence employee choice; (6) given to fulfill an illegal promise of benefits made during the campaign.[54]

Obviously an employer should plan and develop any pay or benefit change independent of union organizing activity. It is equally important to document the design and decisions regarding the changes. One should assume that any decision in this area will be carefully scrutinized by the NLRB, so it is important to carefully document all aspects of the

---

[52] *See American Sunroof Corp.*, 248 NLRB 748 (1980), *enforced in part*, 667 F.2d 20 (6th Cir. 1981); *Honolulu Sporting Goods Co.*, 239 NLRB 1277 (1979), *enforced*, 620 F.2d 310 (9th Cir. 1980); *Micro Measurements*, 233 NLRB 76 (1977).
[53] *NLRB v. Exchange Parts Co.*, 375 US 405, 409 (1964).
[54] *See St. Francis Federation of Nurses & Health Professionals v. NLRB*, 729 F.2d 844 (DC Cir. 1984), *enforcing* 263 NLRB 834 (1982); *NLRB v. Exchange Parts Co.*, supra note 53; *Seneca Plastics*, 149 NLRB 320 (1964); *NLRB v. Arrow Elastic Corp.*, 573 F.2d 702 (1st Cir. 1978); *NLRB v. Rich's of Plymouth*, 578 F. 2d 880 (1st Cir. 1978); *Rupp Industries*, 217 NLRB 385 (1975).

decision. This will not only help in the decision-making process, but will also greatly assist in any defense required. I encourage you to discuss these issues with labor counsel <u>before</u> you embark on implementing changes in pay and benefit programs.

Conclusion

Pay and benefit issues sound a constant drumbeat in most union organizing environments. As tempting as it is to look at these issues as the "key" that will transform your company, ultimately pay and benefit issues are less important than many of the other aspects of an organization discussed in this book. Pay and benefit issues can also divert your attention from other more important areas that pay much bigger dividends in improving morale in an organization

This is not to say that pay and benefit changes will not be perceived positively; they will. It is just important to realize that the positive effects of pay and benefit changes are more short-lived than other changes your organization will make.

At the same time, the attention of your employees can also be diverted by pay and benefit issues, particularly if your organization does a poor job of ensuring external and internal fairness of its pay system. Employees can be distracted from many of the good things an organization is doing in other areas if the "hygiene" factors of pay and benefits are not handled. For this reason your organization may have to clean up pay and benefit issues early to allow employees to focus on other changes.

Attempting to eliminate all pay and benefit complaints is a fool's errand. If your pay system is legally sound (i.e. issues of internal fairness are handled well) and competitive within your defined market for talent (externally fair) you have a good system. You may have to work on communicating it, but you will not make large gains focusing additional energy here. I encourage you to look instead at whether your pay and benefit issues are distracting you or your employees from paying attention to (and appreciating) the other changes taking place in the organization. If not, move on.

Chapter 13

Performance Feedback That Works

"Failure is only postponed success as long as courage coaches ambition. The habit of persistence is the habit of victory"
Herbert Kaufman

What You'll Learn In This Chapter
- The vital importance of performance communication
- How to decide whether formal performance appraisals are right for your organization
- Evaluating whether your firm should tie performance appraisals to compensation
- The three most common problems with appraisal systems and how to solve them
- How to design an effective appraisal process
- Tips to improve informal performance feedback

Failure to communicate regularly with employees about their performance is a common source of employee relations problems. Most organizations rely on formal "performance appraisal" systems as their only means of communicating regarding performance. In the best circumstances, these systems require supervisors to meet with employees formally once every few months; most systems only require a meeting once a year. This is woefully inadequate.

Companies typically spend little effort on performance communication. The process is often viewed negatively by supervisors and managers who are asked to appraise performance of team members.

Particularly when tied to compensation, employees look at the process negatively as well. Lazy supervisors will often avoid any communication regarding performance. If forced to rate employees, these supervisors will rate all employees satisfactory, even where performance levels are not equivalent. In this way, they avoid tough confrontations with poor performers.

Avoiding communication about performance has the paradoxical impact of encouraging poor performance while discouraging high performers. Before discussing the specifics of effectively designing a performance communication system, it is important to discuss why performance should be discussed in the first place.

Should You Conduct Performance Appraisals?
Opinions differ about the importance of doing performance appraisals. This is partly due to the fact that they are rarely done effectively. Some employers feel that performance appraisal systems are inherently difficult to implement. These employers would prefer avoiding them altogether. This is particularly true when the performance appraisals are tied to pay increases.

These employers opt instead for standard raises not tied to individual performance at all. Companies like this, while deserving some credit for being realistic, are missing a great opportunity to improve the performance of both their employees and their company. By failing to tap into the full capabilities of their work force, these companies risk losing high-performing employees to competitors and will never reach their full potential.

There are a number of important reasons for conducting performance communication (whether tied to raises or not). First, making the effort and taking the time for the process motivates employees. An effective performance appraisal program provides an opportunity for employees to compare their performance with what is considered "ideal" performance by the company. Setting performance goals is very motivating to high performing employees and gives direction to lower performers about where they need to improve.

On the other hand, failure to conduct performance appraisals, or doing performance appraisals in an inconsistent or unrealistic manner (i.e. giving all employees satisfactory ratings no matter what their performance level) can be very de-motivating. For example, giving a satisfactory rating to a low performing employee affirms that low performance is acceptable by the company and thus can discount the pride felt by employees about their workplace. High performing employees are de-motivated because they perceive their efforts are unrecognized or not highly valued; their motivation spirals downward to do what it takes to get by and no more. While there are some individuals who are highly motivated internally no matter what system they find themselves in, these individuals are much less likely to be satisfied in a business that places little or no emphasis on good performance.

A second reason to have a performance appraisal process is that it creates another avenue for employee communication. Many of the companies we work with have serious communication problems throughout the company. As discussed in Chapter 7, there are no simple solutions to communication problems. Only a consistent and continuous effort to communicate across many different "channels" will help to relieve problems in a company.

Your communication efforts should include the important channel of the performance communication process. The process can facilitate communication because during individual meetings a manager has an opportunity to communicate with his or her employee about a number of issues. The issues discussed can be about job performance, the employee's role in the company, personal development, and any other important matters on the employee's mind.

These conversations, ideally, should occur on a regular basis. The unfortunate reality often is that they never occur at all. Therefore, the performance appraisal process creates a formalized meeting affording an opportunity to communicate about these issues with co-workers. If the process is formalized, managers and supervisors can be trained to conduct the performance appraisal meeting in a way that not only discusses important performance issues, but also general developmental goals and personal development. These meetings can be highly motivational to employees and are an important piece of a total communications program for a company.

Another vital aspect of the performance appraisal process is that it can enhance the development of managers and supervisors. One reason that many appraisal processes fail is because managers or supervisors do a poor job of executing the performance appraisals. A number of factors contribute to this failure, including lack of training, poor communication skills, or simply lack of priority given to the process. Companies should look at the performance appraisal process as a way to help develop managers and supervisors.

A number of skills are required to deliver effective performance appraisals. Managers and supervisors are required to objectively identify performance traits; track and quantify performance of individuals as well as departmental performance; and effectively communicate performance goals. They are also required to manage performance problems and help identify developmental opportunities for employees. These are critical skills for managers to develop and mastering them can have a dramatic effect on the performance of a company.

A final reason to conduct performance appraisals is to increase the profitability and performance of a company. Some (but certainly not all) effectively designed performance appraisal programs tie individual performance and compensation to the achievement of business goals. If one effectively ties the performance appraisal process to financial and productivity goals, then the improved performance of individuals not only profits them but also profits the company.

Thorny Issue: Tying Performance to Pay
If an important aspect of company profitability is efficient use of resources and a reduction of waste, it is appropriate to appraise the performance of employees on this factor and to tie compensation to the elimination or minimization of waste. In this way, employees are motivated to reduce waste for their own personal gain, which ultimately enhances the profitability of the company. At the same time, employees who pay little or no attention to waste receive no pay raises, which either motivates them to improve their performance or motivates them to leave

the company. In this way, the company can replace poor performers with employees whose goals are aligned with those of the company. The more effectively the performance appraisal process is tied to business goals, the better performing a business will become.

The question of tying compensation to the performance appraisal process is a subject of considerable debate. My personal opinion is that it can be accomplished, but that it is very difficult to do it right. The majority of employers (particularly if they have little experience with performance communication) would be best served by keeping the two processes separate. The problem with tying performance appraisal to compensation is that it highly charges the process. This, of course, is why it is a very good thing to do if it is handled well.

Unfortunately, supervisors (like most humans) want to avoid painful (negative) experiences. Many supervisors feel that telling an employee that their performance is sub-par and therefore they will not be receiving a pay raise is a negative experience (certainly most employees in that situation feel that the experience is a negative one). In an effort to avoid pain, these supervisors will often look for the path of least resistance; "stalling" or avoiding the conversation or "gaming" the process to avoid the conversation altogether. These predictable reactions destroy the effectiveness of any performance communication program.

The same thing happens on the part of many employees. If they know that their raise amount will be announced at the end of the meeting they will pay little attention to anything else until the raise is announced. If the raise announcement comes first they will not hear another word of the meeting.

Even though a skilled supervisor can help to overcome these natural reactions, it is difficult – the average supervisor spends the meeting wondering if the employee is angry with them and the average employee spends the meeting wondering what the raise is going to be. In this environment it is very difficult to have an effective performance discussion. Many employers feel that in this environment it is nearly impossible to have an effective coaching conversation, therefore destroying one of the primary reasons for discussing performance in the first place.

For these reasons many employers decide to divorce pay raises from the performance communication process. As I said before, I have seen effective programs (and ineffective programs) that work either way. The best advice I have for employers is to take a long, honest look at their company and their supervisory team before tying performance communication to pay. While it is the most logical and direct way to connect employees to the key performance requirements of the company, it is also very difficult to implement effectively. In the remainder of this chapter I will discuss systems that tie performance to pay. If you feel that your organization is not ready for this step (or if this is just not consistent with your philosophy) then just ignore the parts about tying it to pay – the remainder of the advice remains valid.

Common Problems With Appraisal Systems
There are three main problem areas common to performance appraisal systems: timing or regularity of reviews; fairness and objectivity of reviews; and a disconnect between performance, compensation and

business goals. In order to design a more effective appraisal program, a company should look at these common faults and avoid them. Each one will be examined in turn.

The timing and regularity of performance reviews is critical to the success of an appraisal program. Employees who receive reviews on an irregular basis, or not at all, can hardly be expected to find motivation in the performance appraisal program. Employees often look forward to the review process, especially when the review is tied to a raise and they feel they are performing well. Employees often think of matters to discuss during the review process. They are disappointed if the review does not occur.

If reviews are deferred or completed in a half-hearted fashion, an important signal is sent to employees about the unimportance of the appraisal process in the company. If reviews are skipped, particularly when raises are delayed or ignored, it becomes very de-motivating and is often cited as a reason employees turn to unions. No matter how well designed an appraisal system, if appraisals are not conducted on a regular basis they are of little use as a motivational tool. Therefore, any effective appraisal system will include tracking of reviews and accountability for regular and consistent delivery of them.

Fairness and impersonal standards for reviews, along with objective performance criteria, are other critical problems with many review programs. Employers, in the interest of simplicity, will often give very subjective criteria for performance reviews since it is much easier to draft opinions rather than impartial and objective standards for conduct. Many times even objective issues are dealt with in a subjective way on performance reviews.

For example, many companies review attendance as a performance-related criterion, without identifying what level of attendance is considered "good" performance and what level is considered "poor" performance. This creates the possibility that two employees with equal attendance records could be rated differently on attendance performance. This creates ambiguity and a number of potential issues.

First, failure to identify fair and objective performance criteria can create a legal problem. If an employee is terminated for poor attendance and other employees with similar or worse attendance records are not terminated, an employer faces a serious risk of a wrongful discharge or discrimination claim.

Elusive criteria also fail to motivate employees to reach specific level of performance with respect to their attendance. If an employee cannot identify a specific level of performance considered good versus a level considered bad, it should be expected that performance throughout the company on that issue will be haphazard. On the other hand, if employees are specifically told what levels are considered good and are then given some motivation (raises, promotions, training opportunities, etc.) tied to the desired level of performance, one would expect to see that level of performance more regularly achieved.

Objectivity is another key. The more subjective a performance criteria, the more likely a supervisor will not know how to rate employees' performance. Subjectivity also increases the likelihood that an employer will be accused of discrimination on a particular issue. Subjective performance criteria create the perfect opportunity for discrimination to occur. In today's litigious society, it creates a basis for employees to claim discrimination even where none exists. For this reason, an objective set of criteria for rating performance is not only more efficient for managers to administer, but also less likely to be subject to discrimination complaints. A very common complaint cited by union supporters is inconsistency in the application of policies and grading performance among managers and supervisors.

Many readers may object at this point, "hey, there is a lot of stuff that we want to talk about that is subjective, like employee attitude and motivation." No question. I certainly would never recommend an employer ignore these issues in performance discussions. However, the biggest problem most employers have is not tying these subjective categories of performance to objective behavior. Just like with your hiring process (discussed in chapter 9), you should train supervisors to identify specific behaviors that lead them to conclude an employee has a poor attitude or is unmotivated.

Instead of saying, "you have a bad attitude" a supervisor could say, "when a coworker asks for your help I have noticed that you roll your eyes and sigh and that behavior can be perceived as if you do not want to help." Picking out specific behaviors to discuss is much less judgmental; you can discuss the employee's awareness of the behavior (if they deny doing it), the impact of the behavior or the reasons for the behavior. It is not subjective. It is something you notice and that you (and perhaps other coworkers) react to. It is something the employee can start to notice and work on, if he or she is so inclined. .

If you tie performance to compensation it must be carefully tied to business goals. Otherwise, the system may not motivate employees to improve the performance of the company. At its worst, a poorly designed performance appraisal system can actually encourage employees to "game" the system and take action contrary to the business interests of the company.

Companies should regularly review their performance communication program with an eye toward business goals that a particular individual can impact in his or her daily job performance. If this analysis is applied to every job performance review criterion within a company consistently, employees will be encouraged and motivated by their own self-interest to help the company reach its business goals.

How To Design Performance Appraisals That Work

A number of strategies are employed when we design a performance appraisal system for an organization. First, we analyze the current performance appraisal system, if any, and identify the problems in that system. While we sometimes will end up starting from scratch with a performance appraisal system, it is nevertheless important to know what has been done in the past and to adopt any pieces of the existing system that work. Many times the problems with a performance communication system have nothing to do with the structure of the system, but merely its implementation.

This review process can use a number of tools. If an opinion survey has been conducted, that is a good place to start. Look specifically at complaints from employees regarding the appraisal system. Catalog these complaints and comments to identify patterns and sources of discontent. If no survey has been done in the company, focus group sessions should be held regarding the performance appraisal process, and suggested improvements to that process.

The next step is to identify the various job positions that are going to be part of the performance appraisal system. Depending on the size of the company and the number of positions involved, these jobs may be grouped according to similarity of tasks involved. The idea is to get a broad picture of the different types of performance criteria that need to be measured and a workable process for this company.

Next one must identify the key indicators of company performance that will be measured. Most successful companies already have a set of key business indicators that they use to judge the performance of the company. This can vary depending on the type of business, but examples include scrap rates, reject rates, quality control measures, number of units produced, and the like. Financial measures like cost per unit can also be used. Customer complaints, on-time delivery and warranty rates are other possibilities.

The ultimate aim is to line up as many objective, measurable business criteria as possible to help drive the appraisal process. This is not to say that other more generic performance appraisal criteria cannot be used. Certainly issues like attendance, team orientation, motivation, attitude etc., can be part of the process. The key is to include as many objective measurements as possible.

The next step in the process is to identify which performance criteria best apply to which positions. Not all positions will have a readily identifiable impact on every criterion listed. Therefore, look at particular job positions and identify how one could best measure that job's impact against the important business criteria identified in the previous step of the process. This step can be the most challenging part of developing the performance appraisal program.

At this step in the process, avoid getting bogged down in questioning what is the most convenient or what applies best across job categories. Simply identify how each job impacts the bottom line. This may require identifying new methods of measuring performance. In companies that are not heavily driven by reporting in numbers, this will certainly be the case. The key to a good appraisal program, however, is the ability to tie the measurable job performance factors to an underlying business goal. This will assist both in communicating the importance of the performance factors to the employees and ensuring that the appraisal process is in fact driving the company toward reaching its stated business goals.

Once the job-specific measurements are identified, the next step in the process is to simplify the appraisal system as much as possible and create forms. In some companies, the same form may be appropriate for all job positions. However, we have found that the best systems have a two-part form. One part of the form may cover generic job responsibilities applicable across the company (attendance, team orientation, - discipline during the review period, etc.). A second sheet includes job-specific performance criteria applicable only to workers in a particular job classification.

With the use of carefully crafted forms, a company can truly drive performance toward its business goals.

The employees also benefit from a very specific, easy to understand road map of how their performance will be judged. These performance numbers should be easily tracked and communicated throughout the year, not just at the time of the performance review. The performance review process should never surprise an employee; he or she should be able to constantly track progress.

Employers often say that this process sounds good on paper, but that the jobs in their company require too much subjective performance traits to use a specific measurement. This, they claim, makes specific levels of measurement for performance goals impossible. We have typically found that these employers are simply too lazy to work through the performance appraisal process in order to find optimal methods. Every job has some type of measurable impact on the bottom line and productivity of the company (otherwise it wouldn't exist). The key is to identify the job characteristics that drive these goals.

The next step in the process (if the organization so chooses) is to tie the performance appraisal program to the compensation system. There should be a clearly stated relationship between the compensation received by an employee and his or her job performance. When tying compensation to a performance appraisal program, I prefer to use a matrix system in which the performance rating is compared to the rate of pay and the individual employee's rate is then compared to the pay range. This method assures a systematic way of determining the performance rating that relates to a specific pay raise. It also allows an employer to ensure that its compensation program is administered in a fair and non-discriminatory fashion.

The final, and vitally important, part of the process is to establish a system that ensures performance appraisals are actually conducted. Some method of tracking dates of appraisals and a system of accountability should be implemented to ensure that performance appraisals and the accompanying communication sessions are completed on time, every time. One method to accomplish this result is requiring review of appraisals before communication meetings occur. Obtaining signed copies of performance appraisals from the employees appraised is another method. Spot-checking the scheduling and follow-through of the communication meetings is a good practice. Finally, a company can tie compensation and performance ratings of supervisors to their success in delivering performance appraisals on schedule to their work groups.

The performance appraisal process is a crucial opportunity for companies to communicate expectations and development opportunities to employees. Failing to follow this practice robs the company of a critical method of improving business performance. Failure to follow an effective appraisal program is also frequently a source of frustration for employees who later turn to outsiders for assistance with employment problems.

Informal performance communication
This chapter has primarily discussed formal performance communication in this chapter while failing to discuss the most important type of performance discussion – informal communication about performance. Formal performance programs are good because they provide regular, "serious" moments to reflect on performance. However, this is not a substitute for regular (by regular here I mean

semi-weekly) informal discussion about performance, both good and bad.

Supervisors and managers who use the formal appraisal process as a substitute for regular informal performance communication are not doing their job. Both types of communication are important. Regular informal communication lets an employee know whether they are "on-track" or if they need to improve. They give the supervisor opportunities to know about things that are concerning employees before they become major issues. It keeps employees and their supervisors connected.

If an employee is surprised by a formal performance review the manager responsible for that employee has failed. The regular communication that occurs on a weekly basis should keep that employee aware of his or her strengths and areas for improvement. Perhaps more important is to talk regularly with employees about their development; classes and training that might interest them, cross-training or mentoring opportunities and "stretch" assignments.

Conclusion
Doing a poor job of communicating regarding performance and development is a common frustration among disgruntled employees. Not surprisingly, efforts made to communicate with employees in these areas can do more than about anything else to improve morale in an organization. Your performance communication program should be among the first areas you consider when identifying projects for your 52-Week program.

Chapter 14

Dispute Resolution and Peer Review

*"It is not he who gains the exact point in dispute
who scores most in controversy, but he who
has shown the better temper."*
Samuel Butler

What You'll Learn In This Chapter

- How dispute resolution programs can often "pre-empt" claims that normally would go to a union organizer, government agency or a plaintiff's lawyer
- Cost reductions that can be achieved through reliance on dispute resolution
- Strategies to reduce the amount of time and energy your firm currently spends on disputes
- Using your dispute resolution program to begin discovery and improve your chances in litigation
- Legal issues to consider when implementing a dispute resolution program
- The main types of dispute resolution programs

People are often surprised to learn that wages and benefits are rarely reasons that prompt employees to turn to unions. The mistaken belief, perpetuated over the years by the unions and the media, is that union employees get a "better deal" than their non-union counterparts. While statistical data is often cited to prove these points, the fact of the matter is that unionized employees, as a whole, receive <u>lower</u> wage and benefit increases than their non-union counterparts. This has been the case for many years.

The fact that high-paying heavy industrial jobs were historically unionized, and some remain so, skews the statistics in favor of unions. However, when looking at "What have you done for me lately?" it is clear the union does a poor job in delivering the wages and benefits now promised.

The good unions readily admit this is true; the toughest organizing campaigns to win are those in which the union does not make big promises regarding wages or benefits. They often will tell employees that in all likelihood they will receive no better pay or benefits by voting in a union. Why? Because, these facts notwithstanding, unions still offer the hope of increased job security to employees in an increasingly insecure work environment.

Many hundreds of thousands of employees have recently faced layoffs and the significant restructuring of their companies. There have been a huge number of mergers that have the financial purpose of combining strengths and eliminating duplicative tasks. Employees who remember the (largely mythical) "good old days" of a job for life as long as you show up for work are frightened by the realities of today's economy.

Unions claim to offer a viable alternative to a work environment where "what the boss says, goes." While the reality is quite different from that painted by the unions, the fact remains that unions do win the right to bargain over significant changes when they win the right to represent employees. While unions cannot normally stop a merger or restructuring, employees are led to believe that the union will ensure greater job security and a bigger voice in their company. Employers who wish to remain non-union must come to terms with this perception, which, justified or not, is a reality in the eyes of employees.

Thus far, we have discussed only the union situation, but other types of third-party intervention should be examined also. Most third-party interference can be successfully avoided using dispute resolution. When employees turn to outside agencies or attorneys to resolve disputes, this is usually not their first step. Most often, employees wish to resolve their disputes internally and without the hassle and grief of going to an outsider.

When employers ignore internal opportunities to resolve disputes or, worse yet, have no effective internal mechanism for dispute resolution, employees are left with few viable options. Workers feel forced to turn to the EEOC, DOL or NLRB (to name only a few) to seek redress. While even these agencies are beginning to advocate alternatives to dispute resolution other than civil lawsuits, any time an employee arrives at one of these agencies the dispute is no longer in control of the parties best capable of resolving it – the employee and the company.

There are several important reasons companies should consider dispute resolution as part of their employee relations strategy. These reasons can be summarized in four categories:
- Union pre-emption
- Reduced expense for most claims
- Quick resolution of most claims
- Cheap discovery for litigated claims

Let's look at each one in turn.

Union Pre-emption

Union pre-emption is an important reason to consider using dispute resolution programs in "at risk" companies. Since unions still persuasively argue that employees need an outside third party for both job security concerns and for grievance representation and settlement, Alternative Dispute Resolution (ADR) subsumes this perceived need for third party intervention. Unions insist that employees cannot trust management and argue that without a neutral outsider employees will never get a fair shake. This attitude is just part of the cultural literacy of workers today (hence the incredible popularity of the Dilbert comic strip). This is due in large part to the unfortunate fact that, for some employers, it is true.

If your company does not have an effective mechanism for employees to get legitimate complaints heard and appealed, the union argument is quite persuasive. The fact of the matter is that the vast majority of collective bargaining agreements contain a grievance procedure, typically including a binding arbitration provision. With a history of over 40 years, these arrangements are well entrenched. There has been recent litigation over whether labor contracts can cover statutory discrimination claims, but the Supreme Court seems ready to allow collective bargaining agreements to cover even these rights, so long as the language is very specific on the issue.

Such a system, affording employees a guarantee that their grievance will be resolved, is appealing. Whether or not the union fulfills other promises made during the campaign, employees latch on to the idea of having someone available to represent them if they are ever wrongfully accused or disciplined for something at work. This gives them a power they would not otherwise have.

Of course, this oversimplifies the grievance machinery in most collective bargaining agreements. In practice these systems can be unwieldy, taking significant time and energy to resolve complaints. Many times employees are left at the mercy of union politics that unfortunately decide many more grievances than neutrals ever decide.

While grievance procedures in collective bargaining agreements are no panacea, they are better than what many employees have in their workplace today. The challenge is to create a system that avoids the disadvantages of grievance handling in many union contracts while improving on the informal "open door" policies so prevalent today.

Therefore one reason for setting up a system for dispute resolution is to take away this "deliverable" from the union. Employees who feel their workplace disputes are handled fairly, where their side of the issue is represented and a decision made in a neutral fashion, will not feel the need to turn to a union for this service. On the positive side, such a system can also be an effective recruiting point for prospective employees. In my mind this is the least important reason for an ADR system, but it is a valid consideration.

Reduced Expense
If your company has ever had the misfortune of becoming embroiled in an EEO charge or other employment law claim, you are well aware of the time and expense involved. There are legal fees, of course, which will typically run into the tens of thousands of dollars even on a run-of-the-mill discrimination claim. These fees often escalate into hundreds of thousands of dollars as the complexity of the claim

increases. In addition, there is lost time and productivity spent in gathering documentation and attending depositions and hearings.

Also present is the frustration of the system, which is just simply not designed for efficient or inexpensive resolution of claims. Even if a claim does not make it to court, being involved in an agency proceeding regularly results in large legal expenses. From the drafting of letters of position to responding to information requests and attending agency proceedings and hearings, many agency claims today approach the expense of a trial.

Mediation, arbitration and other dispute resolution procedures are significantly less expensive than the agency or court proceedings. First, they are less formal and are very often handled without the expense of legal counsel. This alone reduces the costs of claims considerably.

Second, they are typically handled much more quickly. You do not have to wait the 300 days it takes for the agency to act on the claim, only to find out they are issuing a right-to-sue letter that starts the whole process again. An arbitration process is much quicker and cheaper. While companies will spend varying amounts of time and energy preparing for arbitration, the process can be as simple as setting up the arbitrator and holding the hearing. Then, in a relatively short period of time, you receive a decision.

The cost of a typical arbitration (which is generally the most expensive ADR solution on the menu) is significantly less expensive than the simplest agency hearing. If your firm has the capability to handle the hearings and brief writing internally, your costs can be under $10,000 – sometimes significantly less.

Even a more complex arbitration, conducted by a law firm, is still considerably less expensive – if for no other reason than an arbitration does not last as long as the alternatives.

Finally, the awards in alternative forums are typically less extreme than those that go to a jury. This is true even though arbitration agreements should provide the same remedies and awards available through statutory claims (such as attorney's fees and punitive damages) to ensure they will be upheld. You rarely hear of arbitration awards (outside of baseball contract negotiations) for millions of dollars in punitive damages.

The reasonability of arbitration awards is due to several factors. The biggest factor is that there are no juries involved. This results in significant cost savings because juries often base awards on emotional responses to the evidence presented during a trial. By contrast, arbitration relies on an arbitrator or mediator (or panel of arbitrators or mediators) with greater expertise in employment matters who are less likely to be swayed by emotional pleas having nothing to do with the facts of the case.

Another reason, sometimes cited by companies as a disadvantage to arbitration, is that arbitrators and mediators often try to find a "middle of the road" solution to problems. While this can often mean that an employer's decision is not upheld, it also tends to reduce the likelihood of huge, unrealistic verdicts. Therefore, while the awards in the alternative forums may go against companies more often, they also tend to be more realistic.

Quick Resolution

Another reason companies use alternative dispute resolution is to quickly resolve employment law disputes, which can often take years to resolve in agencies or the courts. Alternative dispute resolution resolves disputes much more quickly than other options; mediation and arbitration procedures require time measured in weeks or months. Most employment law cases heard in agencies or courts are lucky to be resolved inside of a couple of years; if appeals are involved, it can easily be three years or more.

There are a number of advantages to resolving disputes quickly. Obviously, the first is that the faster you resolve a dispute, the less your legal fees. Another advantage is that a quick resolution results in less down time for management employees in preparing for and testifying during the arbitration, mediation or other hearing. Finally, if there is a systemic problem that led to the dispute, the employer becomes aware of the issue sooner and can respond more quickly in order to avoid additional liability.

Client Story: Dispute Resolution Makes the Six O'Clock News

One client we worked with was plagued with the typical poor employee relations practices that we usually find in our client companies. Additionally, the company was a very large employer whose every move was a newsworthy event. This company had suffered through two very public union organizing drives in a large pro-union city. It also had been painted, unfairly, as a rogue employer by the union and the press.

Over the course of the year of our association with the company, many efforts were made to improve working conditions and perceptions of the employees about the company. Endeavors included a revision of policies and procedures that had become flash points during the prior organizing campaigns. A number of additional efforts were made to improve employee communication during that year. One of the major complaints of employees, however, related to the fairness and application of policies and procedures by supervisors.

Upon analyzing the complaints, there did appear to be inconsistency among departments in the application of policies. These differences were particularly noted in application of attendance policies. We implemented a proactive process to attack the problem, ultimately employing a combined approach.

First, we revised the policies that resulted in the largest number of complaints, to ensure they were easy to understand and administer. Supervisors and managers were retrained on these policies. In particular a new attendance policy was implemented, which was revised based on a review of what other organizations in the industry were doing.

In addition, a peer review process was developed that would allow a group of hourly employees to review termination decisions made based on issues such as attendance or violation of company work rules. The peer review committee was not allowed to review decisions involving a great likelihood of company liability (such as major safety issues or violations of government regulations). Also, employees had the right to opt for review by management instead of the peer review board, if they so chose.

The peer review board began reviewing termination decisions and, not even a month later, the local news called to do a television story on the procedure. I was not enthusiastic.

In order to heighten interest in the story, the television crew decided to wait until a day that the peer review board was actually meeting. The news crew received permission to interview an employee who was appealing his termination decision. Reporters also interviewed a couple of the members of the peer review board. At the conclusion of the hearing, the peer review board decided to uphold the termination of the employee and the television crew left.

While anxiously awaiting the news telecast, I was filled with dread. I knew we were dead. While I was completely behind the concept of peer review, I was not hopeful that the news crew would understand what we were doing. This was a very "union" town, and our client was not exactly popular. There were just too many angles from which to pound the company.

The news anchors led the story by talking about how our client was letting co-workers decide whether or not to fire an employee. My heart began to sink.

Ultimately, however, the story was a great success for the company. The democratic nature of the process was commended in the story – even by the employee who was terminated!

Legal Issues

Federal law explicitly encourages non-court dispute resolution. The Federal Arbitration Act makes enforceable arbitration agreements.[55]   However, alternative dispute resolution programs, particularly binding arbitration of statutory employment law claims, have come under attack in recent years. The Supreme Court has been asked to review the arbitrability of statutory employment claims several times in recent years, most notably in the cases *Circuit City Stores v. Adams*, 85 FEP 266 (US Sup. Ct. 2001), *Allied-Bruce Terminix Cos. v. Dobson* , 513 U.S. 265 (1995) and *Gilmer* v. *Interstate/Johnson Lane Corp.*, 500 U.S. 20 (1991).

Most recently the Court was asked to prohibit arbitration of employment law claims due to the exclusion in §1 of the FAA from "contracts of employment of seamen, railroad employees, or any other class of workers engaged in foreign or interstate commerce."[56] In *Circuit City Stores* the Court ruled that the text of the FAA does not refer to all employment contracts, only those in the transportation industry.[57]

The Court has also been asked to invalidate agreements to arbitrate employment claims on the theory that states should have the power to regulate employment law claims within their jurisdiction. These claims have also been rejected by the Supreme Court, which has held that congressional intent in the

---

[55] The FAA's coverage provision, §2, provides that "[a] written provision in any maritime transaction or a contract evidencing a transaction involving commerce to settle by arbitration a controversy thereafter arising out of such contract or transaction, or the refusal to perform the whole or any part thereof, or an agreement in writing to submit to arbitration an existing controversy arising out of such a contract, transaction, or refusal, shall be valid, irrevocable, and enforceable, save upon such grounds as exist at law or in equity for the revocation of any contract." 9 U.S.C. §2.
[56] See *Circuit City Stores v. Adams*, 85 FEP 266 (US Sup. Ct. 2001).
[57] *Id* at p. 272.

FAA was to give broad effect to arbitration agreements in all contexts, including employment.[58]

The Court also sees no impairment of statutory rights if they are properly given effect in the context of arbitration. As the court majority noted in *Circuit City Stores*:

> The Court has been quite specific in holding that arbitration agreements can be enforced under the FAA without contravening the policies of congressional enactments giving employees specific protection against discrimination prohibited by federal law; as we noted in *Gilmer*, "[b]y agreeing to arbitrate a statutory claim, a party does not forgo the substantive rights afforded by the statute; it only submits to their resolution in an arbitral, rather than a judicial, forum." 500 U. S. 20 at 26 (quoting *Mitsubishi Motors Corp. v. Soler Chrysler-Plymouth, Inc.*, 473 U.S. 614, 628 (1985)).

Some courts (following the suggestion of some government agencies and plaintiff's lawyers) are limiting the ability of employers to enforce binding arbitration agreements. Many decisions hold that employees are unable to waive their right to litigate employment disputes, particularly if asked to do so in advance of an actual dispute. While this battle is far from over and its details well beyond the scope of this text, there are some general principles worth noting.

Although Congress (with the support of the Supreme Court) actively encourage arbitration of claims over litigation, where specific legal remedies and agencies

---

[58] See *Southland Corp. v. Keating*, 465 U. S. 1, 16 (1984), holding that Congress intended the FAA to apply in state courts, and to pre-empt state anti-arbitration laws to the contrary. See also *Allied-Bruce*, 513 U.S., at 272; see also *id.*, at 282 (O'Connor , J., concurring) (Court explicitly declined to overrule *Southland*).

to enforce those remedies are provided, lower courts and agencies are reluctant to prevent employees from exercising their rights in those forums. While some courts will allow waiver of statutory employment rights, they normally require a number of factors to be present, including: specific notice to the employee of the rights being waived; ample time for employees to read and understand the agreement and policies about arbitration; a fair and neutral forum for hearing the dispute; and provision for the same remedies available under the statute in question (including punitive damages and attorneys' fees).[59]

Despite the favorable Supreme Court treatment of the general concept of arbitration of employment claims, some jurisdictions remain very inhospitable to these agreements. This is also the standard position of the EEOC. Suffice it to say that requiring employees to arbitrate statutory employment law claims, particularly if you require them to do so as a condition of employment before any claim arises, may not hold up in some circumstances.

In addition, many employers fear that employees might get "two bites at the apple" due to this legal complexity. Some argue that, due to the uncertain legal environment surrounding alternative dispute resolution, the likelihood is that an employee will use the procedure and then turn around and sue later for the same set of complaints. In essence, they get to litigate any issue twice and, if lucky, might even

---

[59] See, e.g. *Shankle v. B-G Maintenance Management of Colorado*, 78 FEP Cases 1057 (10th Cir. 1999) (arbitration agreement requiring fee splitting between claimant and employer invalid due to restricting access to forum); *Gonzales v. Hughes Aircraft Employees Federal Credit Union*, 79 FEP Cases 65 (Cal. Ct. App. 1999) (arbitration clause invalid where time limits, discovery rights are less than provided by law and where employer not required to arbitrate); *Michalski v. Circuit City Stores*, 79 FEP Cases 1160 (7th Cir. 1999) (agreement to arbitrate valid where employer agrees to be bound by arbitrator's decision).

recover twice for the same dispute. Many employers who have not thought carefully about the issue dismiss ADR for this reason alone.

Should employers be concerned with these potential problems? As you might guess, my conclusion is that the advantages of ADR far outweigh any potential legal issues or double recovery possibilities. First, it is important to understand that the vast majority of cases resolved through alternative methods work exactly as designed – without a court case. Thus, forcing all aggrieved employees to go into an agency or a court to resolve their dispute is an extreme overreaction. While there may be a case or two where employees want to get into the agency or the court system and avoid ADR, the vast majority will not.

Second, for that minority group of employees who are trying to get to court, you will probably not avoid a lawsuit with them no matter what system you have in place – in other words, you do not save yourself a lawsuit by not using ADR with these employees.

Another advantage of ADR is that you put an additional legal hurdle in front of those employees who are committed to a lawsuit. Many courts and agencies will require the employee to exhaust the ADR system before bringing their claim. This may reduce the attractiveness of the claim to potential plaintiff's attorneys and gives you an opportunity to see the employee's full case before they get to court. In some cases, you may even be able to improve your defense by catching the employee in inconsistencies or outright lies.

Further, the chances of double recovery are quite limited (courts will almost always offset any damage award by prior payments through the ADR system). If there is a great fear of fighting two suits for each dispute, employers can give employees the option of ADR at the time of their dispute. The law is much more settled where employees choose ADR after having knowledge of their claim. In addition, the likelihood of additional suits is very unlikely if the employee volunteers to try ADR in the first place.

Ultimately, there is very little legitimate fear of ADR by either employers or employees. Implementing a system where disputes can be settled early, quickly and inexpensively is an advantage to both companies and employees. Let's face it − employment disputes are inevitable, and resolving them is never simple or pleasant. The quicker and more cheaply these disputes can be resolved, the better for all parties. ADR, while not perfect, is simply the best way to accomplish this.

Which Type of ADR Process Should I Use?

There are a number of excellent options for alternative dispute resolution available today. While I have mentioned each of them, it is worthwhile to describe the processes in detail and outline the comparative advantages and disadvantages of each program. Further, it is good to remember that these dispute resolution processes can be used in combination with one another. For example, many successful programs combine mediation and arbitration and even peer review as steps in their dispute resolution process.

Mediation

Mediation is the least formal level of dispute resolution. Mediation describes the process whereby an independent third party, sometimes an individual in no way associated with the company, listens to both sides of a dispute and attempts to encourage a resolution between the two parties. Mediation within a company can be handled either through a Human Resources department or, better yet, through outside "ombudsman" programs or other formal mediators. The problem with mediating within a company, particularly as a final step, is that the mediator may not be viewed as a neutral party by the employee. A critical aspect of any successful dispute resolution program is that the mediator be perceived as neutral.

Mediation has several advantages. First, it is nonbinding. This means that mediation can be used without significant risk to either party. Mediation has the advantage of getting each party's side of the story on the table early on in the dispute. It also has the advantage of being informal. Informal proceedings normally result in reduced expense and also reduced time commitment.

The main disadvantage of mediation is that many times the dispute remains unresolved. Since mediation is nonbinding in nature, it has very little coercive impact on the parties. If the parties have widely divergent views regarding the facts or a desirable resolution, mediation can be a waste of time for them. Ultimately, however, there is little reason to avoid mediation because of its low cost and effort, and it often moves the parties closer toward settlement of the issue.

Peer Review
There are a number of variations of peer review. The basic concept is that a group of employees is assigned to review specific decisions of the company. This group of employees can be strictly peers (hourly employees review decisions regarding other hourly employees), or a combined board of both hourly and managerial employees. The types of decisions

reviewed by a particular board are also varied. Peer review boards can be very limited in their scope or can be empowered to review literally all termination decisions and other grievances.

Prior to establishing a peer review board, a specific procedure for appeal should be explicitly drafted. The employer should also consider the training of peer board members and the record keeping of appeal meetings. Finally, it is a good idea to give employees the option of appealing directly to management for those who are uncomfortable going through peer review.

The primary advantage of a peer review board is that it empowers employees to make decisions about their employment relationship with the company. Most companies' experience is that the peer review board is often harder on employees than management. Employees also bring a tremendous amount of expertise regarding the day-to-day operations of the company that can be helpful in resolving disputes.

Many employees feel much more comfortable with the decision that is made by a peer review board, even if that decision is the same decision that would have been made by management. Finally, utilizing peer review of management decisions creates a system of checks and balances that many employees seek when they feel that management has been unfair.

However, there are some potential disadvantages to peer review. First, by allowing hourly employees into the decision-making process, confidentiality concerns are raised. These concerns can often be dealt with during the training process. In addition, confidentiality is an important reason to make appeal to a peer review board a voluntary action.

Nevertheless, one can imagine potential liability from poorly trained or untrustworthy review board members freely discussing employment decisions regarding their peers. The same, of course, is true of supervisors or managers who handle employment issues.

Another potential problem (although one I have not experienced) is that peers may unjustifiably overturn every management decision. For this reason it is very important to include fair-minded, conscientious and mature individuals on the peer review board. Nevertheless, if this – like any review system – is abused, it becomes ineffective.

Arbitration

Perhaps the best-known dispute resolution method available is arbitration. Arbitration can be either binding or non-binding. The arbitration process is much like a trial, although instead of occurring in a court of law in front of a judge or jury, it occurs in front of an impartial "expert" in an informal setting.

The advantages of arbitration are many. If the decision is binding, arbitration creates a final conclusion to disputes that, except in the most extreme circumstances, cannot be overturned on appeal. Arbitration proceedings are informal, so there is less expense. The proceedings also require much less time than a trial.

The biggest disadvantage of arbitration is that, due to the potential ease of use, arbitrations can occur much more frequently than court cases. This can result in increased expense for the employer if care is not taken to deal with disputes prior to the point that they are appealed to arbitration. Nonbinding arbitration, while an effective way to bring issues to resolution, can be no more than an expensive mediation in cases where the parties are simply not going to agree. Finally, if the company policy severely limits the remedies or responsibilities of an arbitrator, the holding may not be able to take the place of agency decisions. Thus, the end result could be giving employees two bites at the apple.

An incredible number of opportunities exist for resolving disputes before litigation. Each company needs to examine its own current dispute resolution process and retain what is working in that system. At the same time, it is also very valuable to look at other options for dispute resolution as part of an overall plan. New approaches can be valuable, not only as ways to resolve the inevitable disputes that occur during the employment relationship earlier and less expensively, but also as a way to help employers win those disputes that do end up in front of an agency or in court.

Chapter 15

Planning Your Fifty-Two Week Calendar

*"No date on the calendar is as important as
tomorrow"*
Roy Howard, Scripps-Howard Newspapers

What You'll Learn In This Chapter
- Steps to create a concrete vision of your ideal
  employee relations environment
- Three key strategies for project planning to
  achieve your imagined employee relations
  environment
- Importance of including employees in the
  planning and implementation process
- Utilizing survey data to create your master plan

Now that you know what to do, how will you do it? In
order to transform your employee relations
environment you have to do more than just learn
about best practices or things that other companies
have done. You must not only make concrete actions
aimed at achieving specific objectives but you must
change the conversations that occur throughout your
organization on a daily basis. This chapter will help
you do just that.

First know this: if you fail to plan you plan to fail.
There are a tremendous number of small acts that are
required in order to transform any organization. Not
all of them will be planned – in fact many of them will
be spontaneous. Yet you cannot change conversations

or relationships without first changing yourself, and that we will plan together.

There is no one specific action or program that an employer can implement to turn around a negative culture. Just as it took thousands of actions over a long period of time to create your current employee relations environment, so will it take thousands of actions over a long period of time to improve that environment.

Think of the project like a jumbo jet sitting on a runway preparing for takeoff. At first its engines roar, even though the plane remains still. Eventually the massive fuselage begins to inch forward slowly. Later the jet begins to pick up speed, moving faster down the runway but still moving more like a bus than a plane. However, as more and more momentum is created forces surrounding the plane begin to add to the momentum – forces the pilot has no control over, but forces that exist nevertheless. The plane begins to lift and flies into the air. The engines do not run any faster - in fact they can even reduce their thrust, but the plane continues to fly at great speed.

Like the plane when its engines first start, your plan may at first seem like it is stalled. There will be times that you feel like you are standing still on the runway, even though the engines are going at full throttle. Sometimes you might even feel like you are going backwards. Yet eventually you will see movement. As you gain momentum you will be carried forward and the momentum will build. Soon your employee relations environment will be soaring.

While there are no shortcuts, you can set yourself up to succeed with a good plan. Understand that the plan is more about changing you than it is about changing others. It gives you a bigger picture about where you're going. Utilizing a master plan you can avoid potential sidetracks and inconsistent actions that may derail earlier actions by creating an overall framework for change. Getting the big picture will help you keep things on track when you feel like the plan is slipping.

This chapter will briefly explain the process we use in developing a project plan for transforming an organization's employee relations environment. It discusses the principles of project planning that are utilized and then looks at a typical Fifty-Two Week calendar.

Start with a vision
The first thing any organization must do before embarking on such a mammoth task as transforming its employee relations environment is to envision what exactly the organization hopes to accomplish. I am not talking about a vision statement that is framed and posted on a wall somewhere never to be looked at again. Here you need a vision of your employee relations environment that truly fires up you and your employees. The vision must be something that deep down your organization really wants to see happen.

One way to develop such a vision is through a process called Appreciative Inquiry. This is a process originally developed by a professor at Case Western Reserve University named David Cooperrider. I have adapted it for use in some of my preliminary planning on organization development (for more information on Appreciative Inquiry, see the sidebar in Chapter 5 on the subject).

Appreciative Inquiry is most easily described as focusing on the things that bring life to an organization; what the company does well. The basic premise of Appreciative Inquiry is to spend most effort defining and striving for a high level goal for an organization as opposed to concentrating on the negative aspects of that organization. So instead of focusing on what is wrong with the company, employees are instead encouraged to envision their organization at its best or highest potential state.

Appreciative Inquiry can be done alone (in fact, I'll ask you to embark on a solo journey in just a minute) but it is most effective in larger group sessions with employees. Basically the session begins by asking the group to discuss their personal "highlight" moments in the organization – I like to refer to them as their Sportscenter™ highlights. When did they feel most alive? What is their proudest moment? What did it feel like? Tell the story; make it vivid.

Next they are asked to imagine that they have just awakened from a 5-year slumber; on returning to work they arrive at an organization that has been transformed into their vision of the perfect place to work. The group members are asked to truly imagine all the details they can about this transformed organization, from what it physically looks like to how employees work together to how customers are dealt with and the like. Most important, employees are asked to envision how they have changed. Once people have a clear vision of this organization and their own changes in their mind they then begin to list the various aspects of this organization.

Please take a few minutes and try an appreciative inquiry session for yourself. Pretend like you have just awakened from that same 5-year slumber. Answer the following questions:

- How does the newly transformed organization look in your mind? How do you look and feel? How have you changed?

- Why do you want the organization to look that way? What will it mean to you personally?

- What are the consequences if the organization fails to move toward that vision? How will that impact you personally?

Don't self-censor at this point. Simply brainstorm everything you can about the new organization. Once you have identified these three areas, how you want the organization to look, why you want it to look like that, and the consequences should it fail to reach its potential, you will have made a huge first step in developing your Fifty-Two Week plan.

Next, take your list and start to identify any patterns or common areas in your list. Which items are related to working conditions? Which are related to people-issues? As you begin to group these also start to identify any relationships among items. What strengths can you build on? Are things you listed symptoms of some deeper cause? This will help you begin to envision areas of synergy and also may help you to identify priority areas.

This process is particularly powerful if engaged system-wide. The reason is that it immediately forces a change in the conversations that occur in the organization. This, in and of itself, changes the system. The change will not be permanent, but it is a glimpse of what can happen. As these conversations change on an everyday basis, so too will the organization change. Many organizations use this process to do their visioning.

The advantage of engaging the entire system (all employees when possible, and sometimes also including customers, suppliers, and other key stakeholders) is that you avoid the most common problems with vision efforts – they are the vision of top management and mean nothing to the people who are actually going to be charged with making that vision a reality. Like a pushy parent forcing their child into a sport that is important to the parent and not the child, this strategy is doomed to fail. If you engage in the process using input from co-workers, it also lets you begin to identify a shared vision for the organization on which to focus.

A word on project planning

Since many are not experts on project planning, I include a few words on how to plan a project as massive as your Fifty-Two Week plan. Fortunately, you do not have to be an expert in project planning to be successful, although there are a few pointers that you should keep in mind.

Step 1: Identify Your Employee Relations Objectives

A goal that is in your head is not a goal, it is a dream. While there is nothing wrong with dreams, they make a poor substitute for a project plan on an issue as important as the employee relations environment in your organization. Writing down your goals is the beginning of a plan of action that can be accomplished.

The most important thing that you must do is to identify your objective. This should include as clear a description of your vision of the objective as you can write down. Take some time to literally envision what the work environment will be like once the goal is reached. Try to describe it as vividly as possible.

Next, write down your reason for wanting the objective. Like we did for your overall vision for the organization, identify what it will mean to you personally if this objective is reached. Once again, concentrate on making it as real as you possibly can in your mind. Finally, identify the consequences of failure. What will it mean to you if you fail to accomplish this objective. Once again, envision this as clearly as you can in your mind. Write down what would happen should you fail to accomplish your objective.

The reason for this process is to get you associated with the objective as much as possible. You should go back to these objectives on a regular basis so that you can remember the vision that you identified as well as the reasons you want the vision and the consequences for not achieving it. You may go back and revise these as you think of more information or circumstances change; that is fine. The idea is to try to get as great of a vision as you possibly can in your mind.

Step 2: Prioritize Your Objectives
The next step in the process is to prioritize your objectives. This helps you to identify the highest impact areas for your program and will point out where you should invest your time and energy. This is

a critical step to ensure that your limited resources (in terms of time, money and manpower) are focused in a way to deliver maximum results.

The easiest way to explain the process is to first ask you to take a piece of paper and to draw a giant plus symbol in the middle. Next, draw two lines, a vertical line on the left side of the plus symbol and a horizontal line across the bottom. Next to the vertical line write the words "impact to organization." Under the horizontal line write the words "ease to accomplish."

Now you have four quadrants. The bottom quadrants represent low impact objectives while the top quadrants represent high impact objectives. The quadrants on the left represent more difficult to accomplish objectives while the quadrants on the right represent easy to accomplish objectives. Take a look at the chart below for an example:

High Impact Most Difficult	High Impact Least Difficult
Low Impact Most Difficult	Low Impact Least Difficult

Next you want to begin placing your objectives on this chart in one of the four quadrants. It is actually most effective if you can create the chart on a large piece of butcher block paper or on a large white board. Then you can take each objective and put it on a large post-it note, so you can begin to build a picture of where each objective fits in relation to the others. (I have also done this on Powerpoint slides, which is a little less messy but not as much fun).

Once all your objectives are plotted it becomes clear where you should be investing your energy and resources. Obviously you begin with the "High Impact, Least Difficult" quadrant first – this is your low hanging fruit. As you begin to pick off these issues you will most likely then want to focus on your "High Impact, Most Difficult" and your "Low Impact, Least Difficult" quadrants. If you are lucky enough to get through these issues then you turn your attention to the "Low Impact, Most Difficult" quadrant last.

After completing this process you will have an excellent conception of which issues are most important and most achievable. You will also have developed some momentum for the next step in the planning process.

Step 3: Action Plan and Schedule Your Objectives

Once you have prioritized your objectives, the next step is to break each objective out into specific outcome areas that must be accomplished. Once again, under each of these outcome areas list the reasons, purposes, and consequences for failure for each of the objectives. Many outcome areas will be projects in and of themselves.

Beneath these outcome areas make a listing of milestone achievements that will help to show progress on that area. Do not list every little action that must occur but simply the major milestones that will let you know that you are making progress. As a rule of thumb, if an outcome area has more than 5 milestones, consider whether that outcome area should be split into more than one outcome.

Finally, schedule completion dates for the milestones and assign team members to work on each milestone. Take a look at the sample guide below to get an idea of a project planning guide for one possible objective area.

This list of objectives, outcomes and milestones will guide all your actions during the Fifty-Two Week period. You may want to set up your calendar as a flowchart or timeline. Programs like Project are also good tools for project planning. Some set it up on a special calendar for that particular purpose. Still others keep the project planning portions in a separate binder. Whatever system helps keep you organized is the one you should use.

I have also had success using a daily action planning guide that I look at in the morning and the evening of each day. For example, imagine that you are working on five key objectives based on your survey data and visioning. Say those five areas are:
- ❑ Dramatically improve employee take-home pay by reducing employee insurance premiums, co-pays and/or deductible amounts.
- ❑ Significantly reduce feelings of favoritism by implementing a peer review or dispute resolution process.
- ❑ Create an environment where all employees feel "in the loop" by improving communication between supervisors and employees.
- ❑ Nurture a trusting and high performance environment by giving employees regular and consistent coaching through a performance appraisal and development system.

❑ Build and train the high-skilled workforce we
   need to be a best-in-class organization by
   developing a cross-training program for
   employees.

Now that is a list of some great goals that can really
transform an organization. Next, create a document
that has each of the five areas listed twice. The first
list of five items is entitled "What I will do in each of
my five key areas today." The second list is "What I
did in each of my key areas today."

Next to each item in the list include a couple of blank
lines on which you can write your plans or
accomplishments. Begin each day by looking at your
list and writing your goals in each of the five areas –
they can be very small items, such as making a phone
call or researching a web site. Try to come up with
some small step you can take each day. At the end of
each day review your list and see how you did.

What I have found is that this simple exercise
increases my productivity dramatically. It is easy to
get in a rut and forget about a key action area for a
while – this system doesn't let you do that. Even if
you do just one little thing, you are that much closer
to your objective. Even if you don't do anything about
your objective that day, you are forced to think about
it even if just for a second or two. Eventually it
becomes a habit that becomes a part of your daily
routine – the first vital step to any lasting change.

As completion dates from milestones are hit or
objective areas have been completed, it is important
to celebrate these successes. For interim milestones,
this may be just celebrated among the HR
department. For larger project completions the

celebrations should be firm wide. These celebrations will help keep attention focused on the organization's commitment to improve the employee relations environment and also to help generate momentum toward the completion of still further projects and objectives.

Include Employees or Fail

As you plan activities to help accomplish objectives, always consider how you could include employees. Not every change effort will include employee involvement. However, any activity that requires a change on the part of employees that does not also include those employees in the planning of that change will succeed only by luck.

Let me repeat that because it is so important.

Asking employees to change without including them in the decision and planning for the change will fail unless you just get lucky. You might be able to change management procedures or policies without including others (although even this risks failure) but if you are asking someone to change for your reasons you are wasting your time. Go bang your head against a wall instead – at least the wall won't get mad at you.

This is not saying that all problems can be solved with teams – as we learned earlier, teams are not great at solving many problems. Nevertheless, whether using a team or not, employee input (including the opportunity to object or criticize openly) is essential for a project to succeed on the long term. Forced change can be effective for a short period, but eventually employees will manage a way around the change. Lasting change occurs through the participation and consent of those doing the changing.

Using the survey

Most of our clients utilize the Employee Opinion Survey as the backbone of their planning process. They use the results of the survey to help them prioritize action areas for their Fifty-Two Week program. Most will take the three or four weakest category areas or items from the survey and establish project plans to attack those areas during the first three to four months of their Fifty-Two Week plan. This is a very effective method of planning your year, although not by any means the only method that can be used.

The obvious strengths of using the survey in this way are that it allows you to attack the weakest areas first and gives you a clear road map of projects. The disadvantages of the survey method have been noted before, but are worth repeating here. Surveying can be a negative intervention in the sense that it focuses attention on the problems with an organization and not the possibilities.

Appreciative Inquiry is one method to avoid this difficulty. In addition, the lowest rated items on the survey may not be the items on which the organization is prepared or capable of achieving success in the short term. Therefore, some organizations may choose to concentrate on areas that were not necessarily the weakest rated areas on the opinion survey.

Still others will not have completed a survey or Appreciative Inquiry method at all, but will list their objectives using some other criteria. No matter which method is used, it is important to remember that a survey or other method of discovery is a beginning and not an end. It should be a foundation of your project planning but not a substitute for project planning.

It is important to set quarterly and one year goals in your biggest challenge areas and to regularly review your progress in each of those areas. As mentioned above, you should keep employees informed about your progress in these areas and on the Fifty-Two Week plan itself. Finally, it is an excellent idea to conduct follow-up surveys to help gauge the progress and to identify further areas for action.

Your Fifty-Two Week calendar serves as your guide through your own personal transformation into an employee relations leader. As your daily habits change, so changes the daily interactions you have with your coworkers. The change in those interactions sets off a chain reaction that can ultimately transform an organization. Be clear about your objectives and do something each day to get you a step closer to those objectives. Before long you will be amazed at what you have accomplished.

Chapter 16

Where Do We Go From Here?
Weeks 53 and Beyond

*"Men who are occupied in the restoration of health to
other men, by the joint exertion of skill and humanity, are
above all the great of the earth. They even partake of
divinity, since to preserve and renew is almost as noble as
to create."*
Voltaire

What You'll Learn In This Chapter
- ❑ Some tips on how to keep your 52 Week program on track
- ❑ The six keys to a successful program: assess your position and make a plan; be creative; get help; check your progress; be flexible and expect challenges; celebrate your success
- ❑ Ideas for renewing your program in the years after your 52 Week program

The "52 Week" program is a bit of a misnomer. Becoming an employee relations leader does not end at the conclusion of a year of work. It requires constant effort, forever. It is not a fad program – it must become habit. If you let yourself slip back into bad habits you will end up with the same problems you face today. Care must be taken to consistently and always apply the principles discussed in this book.

The rewards for this hard work are great. Increased productivity, workplace tranquility and profitability to name a few. Just as the negativity of a poor work environment continually reinforces itself, so does the positive feelings that are generated when a group of employees feel connected to the mission of their organization and feel good about the place that they work. This is the mountain that, with your hard work, your organization will scale.

In this final chapter I will summarize the road that you will travel during the first fifty-two weeks and suggest a couple of paths for weeks 53 and beyond. These are the most important steps that you will take to transform your organization into an employee relations leader:

Assess Your Position and Make a Plan
The first and most important step in this process is to figure out where your organization stands today and to map out a plan of attack over the course of the year. Your plan will be customized for your own organization. While many companies share similar problems, none of them share the same individual personalities which will have a significant impact on how particular details of your plan will be implemented.

Nevertheless, there are pathways that have been tread before that provide basic examples of the direction you will want to go in responding to individual problems. This initial benchmarking plan will be something that you will refer back to over the course of the year, both as a means of checking your progress and also as a foundation for the celebrations of success that you will have as you reach your employee relations goals.

Be Creative
Once you have identified the areas that you wish to attack, it is very important to be as creative as possible

in coming up with responses. There are a number of basic responses that have been outlined for you in this text. There are many, many others outlined in other books on this subject. Nevertheless, it is still most important for you to come up with things that you think will work given your particular complement of employees and your organization's own specific mission.

There are many ways to approach employee relations issues that show up as weaknesses in your organization. Often your first attempt to deal with a problem will not be successful. Therefore, it is very important to think of as many possible angles to attack an issue as you can come up with.

Get Help
It is also very important to remember that you are not in this alone. No one person can change an entire organization. In fact, the only person you can change is yourself. Your goal is to create conditions in which your co-workers decide on their own that they want to join with you on your journey.

While in the beginning there may be difficulties in getting people to join you (particularly those who are extremely negative or who have been hurt by the organization in the past) you should be constantly reaching out for assistance. In fact the fastest and most reliable way is to get employees feeling it is their own journey by including them very early in the visioning. This is particularly true of the supervisory and management group. These employees will be responsible for dealing with many of the employee relations issues that will come up.

In addition, it is very important to try to get employees involved in attacking issues that come up in the survey whenever possible. While there are many issues that are not suitable for "team" solutions, there are still many issues where employees can help.

Also, when you decide to use our plan to attack your employee relations issues, don't hesitate to contact us. This is our passion and something that we feel very strongly about. While your particular path will be your own, there are many who have gone before you attacking the same issues.

We would be happy to put you in touch with organizations who have used our model as the basis for their employee relations planning. This gives you an opportunity to bounce ideas off of people who have "been there, done that." While we do not have a formal support network, we do have a number of people who have managed to do a terrific job in improving their employee relations and who are excited about talking to others about their experiences.

Check Your Progress
Don't be afraid to survey throughout the year. While you will not want to conduct a huge 70 plus statement survey more than once every 12 to 24 months, you can always conduct what we call "mini-surveys" on particular issues. You could ask the 10 statements in a category area that you have attacked as a mini survey and compare those results to your earlier survey results. In some cases you may ask completely different questions over issues that come up during the course of the year. You may simply want to conduct focus group sessions or Appreciative Inquiry sessions to gauge your progress.

In any event, it is vitally important to make sure that you are making progress on the issues that you have decided to attack. This also gives you an excellent opportunity to communicate to employees the progress that you have made and to celebrate the changes that have been made in the employee relations environment.

Be Flexible and Expect Challenges

There will be a number of unexpected challenges during the year. It never fails that just at the time that an organization decides to spend significant effort on improving its employee relations, it finds out that its insurance costs are going to increase by 50 percent or that a huge customer is taking its business elsewhere. Challenges like these will come up. These are opportunities for an employee relations leader to really show its stripes. The bottom line is that it's much easier to manage in the good times, but the best companies do a good job of managing even in the bad times.

One should look at these challenges as opportunities to prove the organization's commitment to its employee relations. This normally means concentrating heavily on communicating and explaining exactly why the company is making the decisions it is making. When possible it is also very important to give employees a choice during these difficult times.

In an organizing environment these challenges are all the more evident because there is typically a large group of people looking to put the worst spin on anything that management does and, in the worst cases, looking to sabotage anything that management does. Once you get good at predicting the expected challenges that you will receive from this group of employees, your response will improve. Nevertheless, it is vitally important to attempt a plan as much as possible for the unexpected and to be very flexible when challenges arise.

Celebrate Your Success

The most valuable use of the data that you collect to benchmark your current status and to identify progress during the year is to celebrate progress. The survey results provide an excellent objective benchmark of where your organization is. After several months of working on the issues of concern that come up during the initial survey, it is important to communicate progress to employees.

You should communicate a list of all the actions that have occurred in response to that particular area. Many employers forget to remind employees of things that they have done to respond to issues. This is the biggest communication mistake that you can make.

Employees who are busy working on day-to-day tasks cannot be expected to remember all the different things that management has done over a 6- or even 3-month period of time. In addition, some people take these changes for granted. A particularly negative employee might simply say, "look, that's management's job." However, when given the opportunity it is important for management to remind employees that in the past these things were not handled as expertly, and that based on its renewed commitment to employee relations they now are effectively responding to those issues.

This information also creates common ground for employees. It is a common point of reference that you can and should use to talk about employee relations issues. You should point to the survey results and then identify things that you have done to respond to those particular issues. This should become a habit not just of top management in the organization but, most important, of leads and supervisors.

What's Next?

Once you have completed your Fifty-Two Weeks program, the natural question is what to do from week 53 and beyond. The simple answer is to keep doing what you did during the first 52 weeks.

Each organization is different and their particular answers will depend on how much they have been able to accomplish during the first year. Some organizations conduct a brand new survey and start the process over each year. Other organizations continue working on the initial survey for 18 to 24 months before conducting another survey. Some organizations conduct focus group sessions regularly on the issues that are talked about in the survey and do not conduct a formal survey on a regular basis. The ultimate answer is to do what works for you.

While for many organizations an objective survey is the best method to judge progress, because it provides objective common ground for management and employees to which management and employees can refer, this is not always true with every organization. If you felt the survey process was effective with employees then it should be continued. If employees did not find the survey process particularly exciting, or if it was too negative and not that helpful, then your organization should consider other alternatives like focus group sessions or Appreciative Inquiry.

It is my sincere hope that your organization will be able to find some useful tools in this book to help transform its employee relations environment. There is nothing more satisfying to me than seeing a company whose employees have completely lost confidence in management transform itself into an organization where employees feel connected, proud and positive about their company. It is possible. I have seen it happen in situations that even I felt were impossible. The best news is that it is not a magical or extremely complicated process. It is hard work, but not difficult work. In fact, after Fifty-Two weeks you will find it is one of the most rewarding things you have ever done.

Appendix 1 – Sample Opinion Survey Questionnaire

Statement	strongly disagree strongly agree
1. My work area is always neat and clean.	1 2 3 4 5 6 7
2. I have the opportunity to do what I do best each day.	1 2 3 4 5 6 7
3. I am proud to be an employee here.	1 2 3 4 5 6 7
4. The benefits offered here are fair and reasonable when compared to similar employers in this area	1 2 3 4 5 6 7
5. The most capable employees are always the ones selected for promotions.	1 2 3 4 5 6 7
6. When assigned work I've never done before, I get the necessary instructions to do a good job.	1 2 3 4 5 6 7
7. Generally speaking, my immediate supervisor is doing a good job.	1 2 3 4 5 6 7
8. Communications from top management are adequate for me to know what is going on in the organization.	1 2 3 4 5 6 7
9. I have one or more good friends here at work.	1 2 3 4 5 6 7
10. Today this organization is headed in the right direction to be successful.	1 2 3 4 5 6 7
11. My work area is safe and accidents are infrequent.	1 2 3 4 5 6 7
12. The mission of my company makes me feel my job is important.	1 2 3 4 5 6 7
13. If I had a friend looking for work, I would recommend they apply here	1 2 3 4 5 6 7
14. The benefit plan provides good protection for me and my family in case of accident or illness.	1 2 3 4 5 6 7
15. For a person with my abilities, there are many opportunities for advancement.	1 2 3 4 5 6 7
16. I feel I receive the training necessary to keep me productive in my present job.	1 2 3 4 5 6 7
17. My supervisor listens to my ideas and suggestions when I make them.	1 2 3 4 5 6 7
18. I know what is expected of me at work.	1 2 3 4 5 6 7
19. Someone in management cares about me as a person.	1 2 3 4 5 6 7
20. Top management uses praise and constructive feedback to motivate employees.	1 2 3 4 5 6 7
21. I have the proper materials and equipment to do my job right.	1 2 3 4 5 6 7
22. I find my present job challenging and interesting.	1 2 3 4 5 6 7
23. Morale here is high.	1 2 3 4 5 6 7
24. The best way to get a raise here is to do a good job.	1 2 3 4 5 6 7
25. Around here, "what" you know is more important than "who" you know.	1 2 3 4 5 6 7
26. In the past six months someone at work has talked to me about my progress and development.	1 2 3 4 5 6 7

Appendix 1 – Sample Opinion Survey Questionnaire

Statement	strongly disagree strongly agree
27. My supervisor gives me the attention and support I need to do a good job.	1 2 3 4 5 6 7
28. The channels of communication between employees and management are working satisfactorily	1 2 3 4 5 6 7
29. No one here is ever discriminated against.	1 2 3 4 5 6 7
30. I have great confidence in top management.	1 2 3 4 5 6 7
31. The physical environment (such as temperature, lighting and noise) in my immediate work area is satisfactory	1 2 3 4 5 6 7
32. I have no problem keeping up with my workload.	1 2 3 4 5 6 7
33. The products or services we provide are high quality and worth their price.	1 2 3 4 5 6 7
34. I believe that pay increases are based on performance.	1 2 3 4 5 6 7
35. Whenever possible, promotions are made from within.	1 2 3 4 5 6 7
36. People here are given the chance to cross train for other jobs.	1 2 3 4 5 6 7
37. In the last week I have been praised for doing good work.	1 2 3 4 5 6 7
38. When changes are made that affect how to do my job, the reasons are explained to me.	1 2 3 4 5 6 7
39. I am not aware of any instances of sexual harassment.	1 2 3 4 5 6 7
40. Top management is available to listen to employees.	1 2 3 4 5 6 7
41. Our emergency medical training and facilities are satisfactory.	1 2 3 4 5 6 7
42. I am very satisfied with my job.	1 2 3 4 5 6 7
43. We have a lot of good people here working hard to make us successful.	1 2 3 4 5 6 7
44. The way raises are determined here is fair.	1 2 3 4 5 6 7
45. People here get terminated only for good reasons.	1 2 3 4 5 6 7
46. New employees receive adequate training as soon as they start to work.	1 2 3 4 5 6 7
47. I am able to talk openly and honestly with my supervisor about my work.	1 2 3 4 5 6 7
48. I feel comfortable talking with my supervisor or someone else in management about my personal problems or complaints.	1 2 3 4 5 6 7
49. Our rules and regulations are uniformly administered.	1 2 3 4 5 6 7
50. Top management keeps its promises.	1 2 3 4 5 6 7

Appendix 1 – Sample Opinion Survey Questionnaire

Statement	strongly disagree strongly agree
51. When suggestions are made to improve things at work, those suggestions are given careful consideration.	1 2 3 4 5 6 7
52. If I had to do it over again, I would still go to work here.	1 2 3 4 5 6 7
53. We have an excellent reputation in the community.	1 2 3 4 5 6 7
54. I feel like I completely understand our benefit program.	1 2 3 4 5 6 7
55. My plans are to remain here for many years.	1 2 3 4 5 6 7
56. This year I have had opportunities to learn and grow.	1 2 3 4 5 6 7
57. My immediate supervisor is fair and consistent in the treatment of employees.	1 2 3 4 5 6 7
58. I believe top management knows what employees think about most issues.	1 2 3 4 5 6 7
59. My co-workers are committed to doing high quality work.	1 2 3 4 5 6 7
60. I believe management measures performance fairly.	1 2 3 4 5 6 7
61. Overall, the working conditions here are good.	1 2 3 4 5 6 7
62. The amount of work expected of me is fair and realistic.	1 2 3 4 5 6 7
63. When I tell others about where I work, my comments are always positive.	1 2 3 4 5 6 7
64. Considering the type of work I do, I feel my pay is fair for this area.	1 2 3 4 5 6 7
65. Someone at work encourages my development.	1 2 3 4 5 6 7
66. Everyone here seems to be well trained for their present job.	1 2 3 4 5 6 7
67. My supervisor judges me based on facts, rather than opinions, rumors and personality judgments.	1 2 3 4 5 6 7
68. When management gives out information, I can always believe it.	1 2 3 4 5 6 7
69. Everyone here does their fair share of the work assigned to them.	1 2 3 4 5 6 7
70. When top management becomes aware of a problem it is quickly corrected.	1 2 3 4 5 6 7

The thing I like most about my job is:

_____

_____

If I could change something about my job it would be:

_____

_____

Appendix 2 – Sample Survey Charts & Graphs

Company Name 2003 Opinion Survey - Overall Results

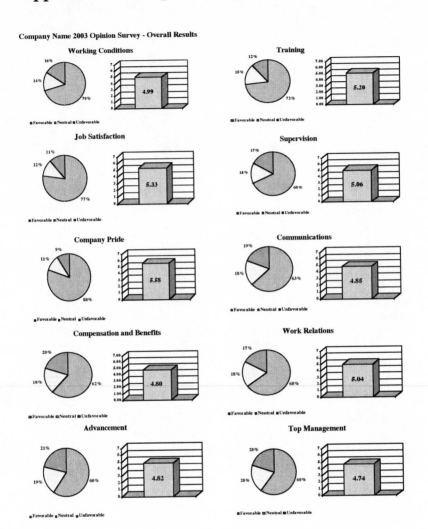

Appendix 3 – Sample Handbook and Policy Statements

Sample Handbook Statements

Welcome to Company Name

We recognize our success depends on a particularly good relationship with our employees. This relationship stresses respect and good faith. We hope these characteristics create an efficient and professional place to work; one in which every person will take pride in his or her job and in our overall continued success. It is hoped that special effort and occasional extra time will be given, when required, out of a feeling that the Company treats its employees in a way that merits their loyalty. In return for your efforts, we strive to provide you with good working conditions.

You have been selected to work with us because of special skills or attributes that you possess. We look forward to utilizing and developing these skills or attributes in a manner that will create a smooth and effective operation; mutually beneficial to both you and the Company.

By joining us you automatically assume your just share of the responsibility for maintaining the high principles and standards that have been established in our Company.

Based on the above philosophy, we try to be as flexible as possible in personnel rules and policies. This booklet is not a "Book of Rules," rather, it has been prepared in order that you might become familiar with the Company; its philosophy, policies and benefits. This booklet should be taken as a clear statement of principles for everyone's benefit. By attempting to avoid any confusion on these matters, it is hoped that we can all work together in a friendly and productive atmosphere. This booklet will also acquaint you with your place and responsibility in the operation of the Company.

Policies will be modified from tine to time to adjust to changing conditions. Your suggestions for modifications will be given careful consideration. Should you have any questions, please feel free to ask them.

About Your Handbook

Each of you, newcomer or veteran, will find this Employee Handbook helpful. It describes the various benefits for which you, as an employee, are eligible and discusses those programs and policies that affect your job. This Handbook supersedes any previous verbal or written policies, statements, understandings or agreements concerning the terms and conditions of your employment at Company Name. Decisions on the interpretation and administration of all Company policies, including those in this Handbook, are the sole responsibility of the Company.

Company Name reserves the right at its sole discretion to amend the contents of this Handbook at any time. Amendments to this Handbook must be in writing and issued by the President of the Company. No other employee, representative or agent of the Company had in the past or now has the authority to amend alter or change the policies set forth in this Handbook or to enter into agreement concerning the terms and conditions of your employment at Company Name. Written amendments will be issued directly to employees or posted on the bulletin board.

Changes in the law may affect the benefits programs described in this Handbook. The provisions of this Handbook do not establish contractual rights between Company Name and its employees. Company Name, in its discretion, reserves the right to add to, modify, amend, alter, reduce or eliminate any or all of the benefits described in this Handbook or which may otherwise be provided, without prior notice to the employees.

At-Will Employment Status

At Company Name, your employment is at will. This means you are free to terminate your employment, at any time, for any reasons, with or without cause, and Company Name retains the same rights. No amendment or exception to our at-will employment policy set forth above can be made at any time, for any reason, except by the President of the Company and it must be in writing, directed to you personally, and signed by him. Any oral statements concerning your employment status by any person will not, and cannot, override the above statement.

Open Door

Our goal at Company Name is to provide a pleasant working environment for all employees. This is achieved by developing and maintaining a cooperative working relationship among employees based on mutual respect and understanding. We recognize the need for procedures that will allow employees to call attention to work-related matters that they feel need correction.

We strongly endorse an "Open Door" Policy where an employee has the right to meet with any supervisor or Company official of his/her choice to discuss such matters of concern. At the same time it is an important part of our company philosophy to encourage problem solving at the lowest possible level of the organization. Therefore, while you are encouraged to freely discuss issues with any member of management, you will always be asked to begin problem solving with your immediate supervisor. If you are uncomfortable working out an issue with your immediate supervisor, you should speak to their supervisor.

Company Name Open Door Policy is in effect during each working day. The Company's success is built on the free exchange of ideas, creative management and the identification of problem areas and their quick resolution. Direct day-to-day communications with your supervisor provides you with an opportunity to let Company Name know of your problems, suggestions, or ideas.

Employee Relations

Company Name's policy has been and will continue to be an open company/open door policy under which all employees have the right to deal directly with their supervisor and other Company officials with reference to all working conditions.

It has not been necessary in the past, and it is not now necessary, for Company Name's employees to belong to any labor organization in order to work for this Company. No employee is required to obtain any other person or organization to represent him/her in the presentation of complaints, problems or questions of application of working policies in discussion with management.

As a result of Company Name's Employee Relations Policy, it is our belief that a labor organization would not work for the benefit of our employees, but rather to their harm. We prefer to deal directly with you to resolve any issues of concern regarding your work here at Company Name and believe that outside third parties can only impair our ability to do this. It is, therefore, our intention to oppose unionism by every proper means and in particular by proper treatment of you and all of your fellow employees.

Sample Policy Statements

COMPLIANT RESOLUTION POLICY

Employees are encouraged to bring their complaints about work related situations to the attention of management. Employees will be provided with an opportunity to present their complaints and appeal decisions by management through a formal complaint procedure. All complaints will be resolved fairly and promptly.

1. A complaint may be defined as an employee's expressed feeling of dissatisfaction concerning conditions of employment or treatment by management, supervisors, or other employees. Examples of actions which may be cause of complaints include, but are not limited to:

    (a) Application of agency policies, practices, rules, regulations, and procedures believed to be to the detriment of an employee;
    (b) Treatment considered unfair by an employee, such as coercion, reprisal, harassment, or intimidation;
    (c) Alleged discrimination because of race, color, sex, age, religion, handicap, national origin, sexual orientation, military reserve, or veteran status, marital status, or any other non-merit factor; and
    (d) Improper or unfair administration of employees' benefits or conditions of employment such as paid time off, fringe benefits, promotions, retirement, holidays, performance review, salary or seniority.

2. No employee shall be penalized for using the agency's complaint procedure. A complaint must be brought forward as soon as it might reasonably have become known to exist. In the event a complaint arises, the employee must submit it to his or her supervisor within five working days. Supervisors are responsible for ensuring that the complaint is fully processed as expediently as possible. The time limit at any stage of the complaint procedure may be extended by written mutual agreement of the parties involved in that step.

3. Any complaint presented shall be on the form prescribed by the Human Resources Manager. It must be dated and signed by the employee presenting it. When a written complaint is presented, the agency's representative shall provide a dated and signed receipt for it at that particular step. Any decision rendered shall be written to the employee and shall be dated and signed by the agency's representative at that step.

4. Any complaint filed shall systematically follow the procedure as outlined below, and shall refer to the provision(s) of agency policy, practice, procedure, rule or regulation alleged to have been violated, and shall adequately set forth the facts pertaining to the alleged violation.

5. **STEP 1**- The complaining employee shall present a complaint in writing to his or her immediate supervisor. Discussions will be informal for the purpose of settling differences in the simplest and most direct manner. The immediate supervisor shall reach a decision and communicate in writing to the complaining employee within two working days from the date the complaint was presented. A copy of the complaint and the decision rendered will be forwarded to the Department Director, Human Resources Manager, and the Executive Director.

STEP 2 - If the complaint is not settled in the first step, the complaining employee shall, within three working days, forward the written complaint to the Department Director. The Department Director shall, within five working days, meet with the complaining employee to determine the facts of the case. The Department Director shall notify the complaining employee of his or her decision, in writing, within three working days following the date of the meeting. A copy of the complaint and the decision rendered will be forwarded to the Human Resources Manager and Executive Director.

STEP 3 - If the complaint is not settled at Step 2, the complaining employee shall, within three working days, forward the written complaint to the Human Resources Manager. The Human Resources manager shall meet with the complaining employee within five working days after receipt of the complaint. The Human Resources Manager shall ascertain the facts and forward recommendations to the Executive Director within three days after the meeting. The Executive Director shall have five working days to consult with any of the parties involved and render a decision in writing to the employee.

The decision of the Executive Director at Step 3 shall be final and binding on the parties, without further right to appeal.

6. Employees directly supervised by the Executive Director shall present a complaint in writing to the Executive Director. Discussions will be informal for the purpose of settling differences in the simplest and most direct manner. The Executive Director shall reach a decision and communicate it in writing to the complaining employee within two working days from the date the complaint was presented. A copy of the complaint and the decision rendered will be forwarded to the Human Resources Manager and to the Vice President of COMPANY NAME. If the complaint is not settled, the

complaining employee shall, within three working days, request in writing a meeting with the Vice President of COMPANY NAME. A meeting will be held as soon as practical and an answer in writing will be provided within ten working days following the date of the meeting. The decision shall be final and binding on the parties, without further right to appeal.

5. A complaint not advanced to the next step within the time limit provided shall be deemed permanently withdrawn, and as having been settled on the basis of the decision most recently given. Failure on the part of the agency's representative to answer within the time limit set forth in any step will entitle the employee to proceed to the next step.

Peer Review Policy

I. Purpose
To provide a neutral, non-management body for employees to address grievances regarding decisions to suspend or terminate employment.

II. Scope
This policy applies to all non-exempt employees.

III. Policy
All recommendations to suspend or terminate an employee, except where that employee is being suspended or terminated for gross misconduct, may be appealed to a peer review board for final and binding determination of the issue.

IV. Definitions

A. Gross Misconduct: Gross misconduct is an act which: risks death or serious injury to a guest or another employee or risks significant legal liability to the company. The Director of Human Resources shall determine, based on the facts of each case, whether an act is Gross Misconduct under this policy. It is understood that, whenever possible, cases should be appealable to the Peer Review Board. The Company will not allow an employee to appeal a termination for gross misconduct to a peer review board.

B. Peer Review Board Panel: A five member panel of employees randomly selected from a pool of previously qualified candidates who is designated to hear cases under this policy.

C. Non-Departmental: Employees outside of an aggrieved employee's own department.

D. Aggrieved Employee: Any employee who appeals an employment decision under this policy.

V. Procedure
Any employee who wishes to appeal a suspension or termination recommendation to the Peer Review Board shall do so according to the following procedure:

A. Right to Appeal: When an employee is notified by Human Resources of the decision to suspend or terminate employment, that employee shall be told of their rights of appeal, if any, under this policy.

B. Five Day Notice/Waiver: An employee who wishes to appeal a decision to terminate employment shall notify the Human Resources Department within 5 days of their notification under Section A. Any employee who fails to notify the Human Resources Department in writing of their intention to appeal this decision shall waive any right to peer review under this policy and the final decision of management shall stand, subject to review by the Director of Human Resources and the General Manager.

C. Convening Peer Review Panel: Once the Human Resources Department is notified of an employee's intent to appeal, it shall convene a five member panel of the Peer Review Board according to the following policy:

1. Any non-exempt employee who wishes to be eligible to participate on the Peer Review Board shall be allowed to do so, so long as they meet the following conditions:

(a) They participate in a one-hour training session explaining the process and procedure of Peer Review Board meetings.

(b) They submit their name to the Human Resources Department as being eligible to sit on the Peer Review Board.

(c) They are an employee in good standing in their department and not on final warning or suspension.

2. The Human Resources Department shall refer all appeals to the Peer Review Board, except for suspensions and terminations for gross misconduct or because of loss of that employee's gaming license.

3. The Human Resources Department shall pick five board members and two alternates according to the following procedure:

(a) A list of all eligible Peer Review Board members shall be kept in the Human Resources Department, listing each eligible employee's name, badge number and department.

(b) The name of each eligible Peer Review Board employee who is from the same department as the employee filing the appeal shall be removed from the list for the purposes of this one appeal.

(c) The remaining names shall be placed on individual pieces of paper and placed into a box.

(d) A representative of the Human Resources Department and at least one other witness, shall pull seven slips of paper from the box. One or more of the other witnesses shall be shown the names of the seven persons chosen. The Human Resources representative shall then write down the names of the five board members (the first five names chosen) and the two alternates (the last two names chosen) and the witness(es) shall attest that those were the seven names chosen.

(e) The five board members and two alternates shall be notified of a time and date for the hearing on the matter. The time can be agreed upon by the board members, but in no event shall the hearing occur more than seven days from the date the names are drawn unless prior written authorization is given by the aggrieved employee to hold the hearing more than seven days from the date names are drawn.

(f) The five board members, two alternates, department manager and the aggrieved employee shall be notified of the time and date of the hearing by the Human Resources Department. Notification shall be by phone and/or certified mail.

D. Hearing Procedure

1. On the agreed date, time and location the five board members and two alternates shall meet. It shall take five board members to create a quorum, and if one or two of the board members is absent the two alternates shall be placed on the board. Should there be less than five board members for any reason, the hearing shall be rescheduled.

2. The Board shall meet with a representative of the Human Resources Department prior to the hearing. The board shall select a chairperson for that

hearing. The board shall also be given a brief summary of the facts of the case from the Human Resources representative. This summary shall be in writing and will be given to the aggrieved employee at the time of the hearing. The chairperson will call the hearing to order and the aggrieved employee will be asked to enter the room.

3. There shall be no formal procedural rules, although the hearing shall follow the basic outline provided in this policy. The aggrieved employee will be given an opportunity to state their case to the board. The board and alternates shall be given an opportunity to ask questions of the employee. The aggrieved employee and the company representative shall not be allowed to cross examine each other directly, but they shall be allowed to suggest questions to be asked by board members if they so choose. Board members shall not be required to ask questions suggested to them. Witnesses may also be suggested by the aggrieved employee or company representative. The Board may, but is not required, to call any witnesses. No non-employees shall be allowed in the meetings and employees who bring cases before the board shall be required to represent themselves.

4. A representative of Human Resources shall also be present at the hearing to take notes on the proceeding and to be available as a resource regarding questions on company policy. This representative may also act as the company representative in some cases.

5. Once the aggrieved employee and the company representative have been questioned by the board, the board will excuse the aggrieved employee, the company representative and the Human Resources Department representative. The board and alternates shall then deliberate on the case until a decision is reached. Alternates may participate in the deliberations but may not vote on the outcome.

6. All decisions will be by a simple majority of the five member board. All decisions of the Board shall be final and binding on the company and the aggrieved employee. No board member shall discuss cases with unauthorized personnel nor shall any employee, other than the Human Resources Department representative, speak to the Board regarding the case.

Appendix 4 – Sample Exit Interview Form

JOB CONTENT

1.What factors contributed to your accepting a job with COMPANY NAME? Have your feelings changed?

2.Did you understand the job expectations when you were hired?

3.Did you receive sufficient training to meet those expectations? Did you know how or where to get information you needed to succeed in your job?

4.How would you rate your own performance on the job?

COMPANY AS A PLACE TO WORK

5.How would you rate the following aspects of your employment here?

Aspect of Employment	Excellent	Good	Fair	Poor
Opportunity For Advancement				
Performance Appraisals				
Physical Working Conditions				
Your Salary				
Vacation/Holidays				
Other Company Benefits				
Feeling of Belonging				

6.If you were leading this company, what would you do differently?

7.What made your employment enjoyable?

8.What would make you interested in returning to work at COMPANY NAME?

QUALITY OF SUPERVISION

9.How would you rate your supervisor in the following areas?

Supervisory Area	Excellent	Good	Fair	Poor
Demonstrates Fair & Equal Treatment				
Provides Appropriate Recognition				
Resolves Complaints/Difficulties In Timely Fashion				
Follows Policy & Procedures				
Informs Employee of Matters Relating To Work				
Encourages Feedback				
Is Knowledgeable In Own Job				
Expresses Instructions Clearly				
Develops Cooperation				

10.If you came back to work for the company, would you work for the same supervisor?

<u>REASON FOR LEAVING</u>

11. Are you leaving for a similar job?

12.How is your new job different from the old one? Are you staying in the same industry?

13. What part does salary play in your decision to leave?

14.What made you begin looking for another position, or, if appropriate, what made you listen to the offer to interview for another position?

15.What could COMPANY NAME have done to prevent you for leaving?

16.If you are going to another job, what does the job offer you that your job here did not?

Employee

Signature_____Date_____._____

Appendix 5 – Sample 52 Weeks Plan/Presentation

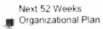

Next 52 Weeks
Organizational Plan

Company Name

Company Name as Leader

- Company Name often leads the corporation in the implementation of new and innovative processes
  - Process Safety
  - ISO-9002
  - Skill Based Pay
  - Product development and the ability to quickly react to customer needs

The Challenge

- To create an environment in which each employee feels appreciated and can perform at the highest level possible.
- To lead the company by being a model for improving our organization.
- To build trust between management and employees.

Organizational Review

- Employee Opinion Survey
- Review of plant performance
- Review of company policies and procedures
- Wage and benefit survey of local competitors for talent and top performing plants in industry

Next 52 Weeks Plan

- Continue to improve communication
- Improve supervisor's and manager's role in performance management
- Implement 3 year compensation plan based on productivity or pfa. ?
- Improve working conditions and reduce physical workload where needed and possible

Communication

- Conduct communication survey
- Hold monthly training meetings for each shift
- Plant manager to hold individual meetings with employees
- Monthly "Breakfast with the Manager" for cross-functional communication

Performance Management

- Train managers and supervisors on coaching skills
- Include performance and development discussions as part of regular review
- Hold managers accountable for the development of their direct reports

3 Year Compensation Plan

- Reward employees for performance, dedication and response to change
- Exceptional work ethic
- Expect each employee will contribute to facility productivity in future
- Evaluated each job for:
  - Complexity
  - Level of self-direction required
  - Compared to our employment market and industry

Wage Survey

Job Title	A	B	C	D	E	F	G	H	I	J	Avg
Supervisor	23.21	21.18	19.61	18.23	17.85	20.07	N/A	19.85	18.21	8.16	19.68
Operator A	N/A	20.42	18.84	18.00	18.80	18.95	18.62	18.74	18.03	17.28	18.46
QC	17.21	17.64	18.81	17.38	17.04	21.10	18.35	21.29	17.85	16.94	18.39
Shipper	18.79	17.01	18.81	18.38	17.04	16.00	16.59	18.02	18.01	17.13	18.25
Warehouse	16.91	18.12	18.57	18.17	17.14	15.13	18.14	18.36	16.42	19.67	17.69
T & R	15.57	18.59	15.65	16.88	16.17	16.21	19.24	21.57	16.55	20.01	18.74

Annual Increase

- Beginning in November overall average hourly rate of pay increase by 3.5% each year for next 3 years.
- Yearly increase plus rate adjustment puts Company Name at or near the top of our industry.
- Maintain superior benefits in the industry.
- Dependent on the facility's continued level of productivity

Improve Work Conditions

- Review physical requirements of all job tasks
- Prioritize capital expenditures in areas that increase productivity while reducing physical workload

Thanks ... and our challenge

- This program recognizes of our hard work and our place as one of the top performing plants in our industry.
- We can't rest on our past accomplishments. We have to continue to improve, work hard and exceed expectations.

Index

A

Activity Profile.. x, 49, 55-56
ADR (alternative dispute resolution) 219-221, 228-230
Advancement 10, 52, 73, 90, 92, 97, 99, 142, 147, 257, 270
Appreciative Inquiry 68, 75-77, 237-238, 247, 252, 255
Arbitration............. 225, 233

B

Bensinger, Richard..... 19-20

C

Card Check
See Union Organizing
CEO........vii, 29, 33, 161, 163
CFO.................................... 5
Change ...vi-ix, 2-12, 17, 20, 27, 29, 43, 50, 63, 67, 71, 75, 84-85, 90, 92, 95, 118, 124-126, 138, 147, 152, 158, 168, 176, 182-185, 197-199, 217, 235-241, 245-248, 251-254, 258-259, 263
Collective Bargaining . 4, 8, 12, 21, 33, 37, 41, 59, 65, 83, 145, 148, 219-220
Communication ....xi, 2, 10, 31, 41, 46, 52, 54, 61-62, 65, 80-81, 86, 89, 98, 101-127, 135, 158, 182, 200-206, 210, 214-215, 224, 244, 254, 258

and Grapevine see Grapevine
and Multiple Channels 108

D

Dispute Resolution .....xi, 6, 10, 27, 54, 60, 88, 115, 119, 123, 143, 209, 216, 219-233, 244, 264-266
see also Peer Review

E

Early Warning Signs 18, 24-26, 55
Emotional Intelligence. 93-94
Employee Relations .. v-viii, 1-6, 12, 16-17, 24, 35, 38, 43, 48-49, 60, 62, 72, 77-78, 89-92, 95, 103-104, 113, 132, 151, 166, 179, 185-186, 200, 218, 223, 235-237, 240, 245, 248-255
Employment Misery Index x, 49, 51
Exit Interviews 185, 187-189
Expectations...... 2, 71, 100, 104, 174, 214, 270

F

Fear......................37-38, 4,
Focus Groups 71

G

Grapevine 105-107, 110, 119, 195

H

Habit.... vii-ix, 64, 174, 178,
200, 245, 248-249, 254
Handbook ....xii, 23-24, 27,
31, 53-54, 74, 115-119,
170, 173, 262-263
High Road 39-41
Human resources 2, 6-7,
10, 46, 100, 174

I

Interviews.................68, 187

L

Leadership.. vii-viii, 19, 28,
37, 65, 70, 92-93, 122-
123, 133
Legal Issues 61, 82, 145,
176, 182, 185, 196, 216,
225

M

Management .. 1-10, 14, 20-
23, 26, 28, 37, 40-47, 50-
53, 63-77, 83, 89, 91-96,
100-113, 122-124, 127,
131, 139-143, 146-150,
156, 159, 183-184, 188,
190, 194, 219, 223-224,
228, 232-233, 240, 246,
251, 253-259, 263-264,
267, 278
Mediation 221, 230-231
Motivations ....x, 35

N

NLRB ... x, 3, 14, 18, 22, 30,
49-50, 56, 82-87, 113,
140, 145-152, 182, 194,
197-198, 218
and Election Campaign
.3-4, 22, 25-26, 31, 42,
49, 50, 56, 58, 63, 86,
124, 151, 154, 197

O

Opinion Survey .... x, 43-47,
51-52, 55, 60-90, 96, 110,
119, 123-125, 128, 142-
145, 176, 185, 190-193,
210, 235, 244-247, 252-
257
and Focus Groups........ 71
and Interviews 68, 187
Organization development ..
2, 75-77, 237
Organizing......... see Union
Organizing
Orientation xi, ...11-12, 98,
103, 118, 121, 166-174,
181, 211-212, 264

P

Pay and Benefits xi, 6, 9, 11,
25, 27, 29, 33, 37, 52-54,
73, 84, 86, 93, 95, 103,
105, 116, 119-125, 139,
142, 145-148, 168, 174-
201, 204-206, 210, 213-
217, 244, 257-264
Peer Review ....xi, 189, 216-
234, 244, 267-268
Performance 187, 200-207,
210-215, 244
Policies xi, 10-11, 27, 43-44,
54, 72-73, 85, 90, 105,
115-120, 147, 167-170,
174, 194-195, 209, 220,
224, 227-228, 246, 262-
264
Pragmatism 37, 41
Pre-emption .... xii, 1, 15-16,
218-219

Project Planning.. 235, 237, 240, 243-244, 247

R

Recognition˙....... xi, 176, 270
Rewards .7, 20, 22, 95, 103, 176-184, 195, 249
Recruiting 11, 121, 151, 163-166, 220
   and Interviewing 23, 68, 151-152, 155-161, 166, 185, 188-189, 225, 270
   and Screening 11, 156, 161-163
Regulatory Compliance ...x, 49, 53
Relationship ....vii-ix, 2, 17, 28, 45, 56, 92, 99, 112, 173, 236, 239, 248
Relevance............ 37, 42, 44

S

Safety 11, 53-55, 59, 83, 89, 128, 132, 137-143, 147-148, 174, 224, 257
Screening .....xi, 151, 153, 161
Size of Company...............57
Supervisor .. 5, 6, 11-15, 24-28, 43, 52-55, 63, 71-77, 80, 85-86, 90-104, 107, 115-127, 148, 152, 158, 167, 170-174, 177, 180, 183, 188, 195, 200, 203-209, 214-215, 224, 232, 244, 251, 255, 257-259, 263-265, 270

T

Teams 47, 77, 98, 103, 128-129, 132-137, 142, 145-150, 180, 246

Third Party Intervention. 4, 13, 16, 20, 36, 43-45, 49-57, 60, 72, 84-86, 182, 219, 230
Training ..10-11, 14, 44, 54-55, 73, 90, 94, 97-101, 108, 118-121, 132, 144, 161, 171-174, 203, 208, 215, 232, 257-258, 268, 270, 280
Transformation ...vi, 16, 248
Trust .2, 17, 37, 42-44, 107, 124, 191, 194, 219

U

Union ... vi, 1-43, 48-66, 77, 81-88, 107, 112-113, 120, 122, 124, 139, 143, 145, 152-155, 167, 182-183, 186, 197-198, 209, 216-225, 228
   and Card Check....... 7, 20
   and Early Warning Signs 18, 25-26, 55
   and Organizing . vi, 2-13, 18-43, 48-50, 53, 55-65, 73, 77, 81-87, 107, 112-113, 120, 123-128, 139, 143, 145, 151-154, 167, 182, 186, 197-198, 216-217, 223-224, 253
   and Pre-emption .1, 218-219
Union-Free x, 1, 4, 7-15, 22, 31, 34-38, 41, 47-48, 168, 184
   and Motivations.... 9, 14, 28, 35-48, 57, 61, 65-66, 77, 95, 174-187, 194, 202, 207-211, 228-230

V

Vulnerability x, 3, 7, 49, 53, 55, 58
and At-Risk ...1, 8, 9, 10, 11, 113, 185

W

Work Environment vi-ix, 1-4, 11-14, 37-39, 42-43, 47-52, 61, 66-68, 80, 104, 108, 112, 125, 140, 144-145, 150-151, 156, 160-162, 167-168, 171-173, 177, 183, 206, 217, 228, 235-237, 240-241, 244-245, 250, 253, 255, 258, 263

About LRI Management Services, Inc.

LRI Management Services, Inc. is a full service labor relations consulting firm dedicated to the operational freedom, workplace tranquility and profitability of our clients.

About Phillip B. Wilson

Phillip B. Wilson, Esq. is Vice President and General Counsel of LRI Management Services, Inc. He is a nationally recognized labor and employee relations authority. Prior to joining LRI, Mr. Wilson represented companies nationwide with the Chicago law firm Wessels & Pautsch, P.C. Mr. Wilson assisted clients in all areas of labor and employment law including union representation matters, collective bargaining negotiations, arbitrations and decertifications. Mr. Wilson was also Director of Human Resources for a $65 million annual revenue gaming corporation employing over 1,200 people.

Mr. Wilson received his Juris Doctor degree from the University of Michigan Law School. Mr. Wilson completed his undergraduate degree *magna cum laude*, Phi Beta Kappa, from Augustana College.

Mr. Wilson is the author of numerous books for both unionized and non-union employers. He has also written numerous articles and book chapters relating to a broad range of workplace issues, including a chapter in the American Bar Association's treatise on The Fair Labor Standards Act. Mr. Wilson has been invited to testify before Congress numerous times on union financial reporting and labor law reform. Mr. Wilson is admitted to the Illinois Bar and is a member of the American Bar Association, the Society of

Human Resource Management, the Industrial Relations Research Association and a number of other professional organizations.

Other Publications by Phillip B. Wilson

- *Managing the Union Shop*, Broken Arrow, OK: Labor Relations Institute.
- *How to Investigate Grievances*, Broken Arrow, OK: Labor Relations Institute.
- *Model Contract Clauses*, Broken Arrow, OK: Labor Relations Institute.
- *Model Reprimands for the Union Shop*, Broken Arrow, OK: Labor Relations Institute.
- *We Won Our Election, Now What?* Broken Arrow, OK: Labor Relations Institute.
- *The Case For Reform of Union Reporting Law: How Financial Transparency Could Have Prevented ULLICO and Other Abuses*, Washington, D.C.: Labor Policy Association.
- *Union Corruption: A Study of the Problem, Its Sources, and Its Remedies* Fairfax, VA: National Legal and Policy Center.
- *Conquering the Enemy Within: The Case for Reform of the Landrum-Griffin Act*, Journal of Labor Research Volume XXVI, No.1
- *Current Section 13(b) Exemptions From the Overtime Requirements of the Act in The Fair Labor Standards Act* in *The Fair Labor Standards Act* (Chapter Contributor, Ellen C. Kearns, ed., Washington, D.C.: The Bureau of National Affairs).
- *Reporting Union Finances* in Labor Watch, Washington, D.C.: Capital Research Group.

Order these publications for <u>your</u> team today!

- ❑ *Comprehensive*—most labor topics covered
- ❑ *Thorough*—written by a labor lawyer
- ❑ *Handy*—designed to be <u>used</u>, not sit on a desk
- ❑ *Understandable*—no jargon, covers key concepts
- ❑ *Inexpensive*—beginning **under $10** each

Also Available **How to Investigate Grievances – Model Contract Clauses – Model Reprimands**

CALL (800) 888-9115, **FAX** the form below to (918) 455-9998 or order online at www.lrionline.com

YES! Send me the following tools for my team	Copies	Price	Total
Managing the Union Shop – 74-page guide for supervisors (1.00 ea. shipping).		$9.99 + shipping	
How to Investigate Grievances – 68-page guide for supervisors (1.00 ea. shipping).		$9.99 + shipping	
Training Kit – 3 DVDs, Powerpoint slide presentation for both *Managing the Union Shop* + *How to Investigate Grievances* and all 4 Union Shop Titles ($25.00 ea. shipping)		$2,499 + shipping	
Model Contract Clauses – Over 200 model clauses (strong company and union proposals) plus drafting guide (5.00 ea. shipping).		$39.99+ shipping	
Reprimands for Union Shops –Nearly 100 sample letters of reprimand; document problems and win grievances ($5.00 ea. shipping).		$29.99 + shipping	
The Next 52 Weeks: Transforming Your Company Into an Employee Relations Leader (5.00 ea. shipping).		$39.99+ shipping	

Name	
Company Name	
Address	City/State/Zip
Phone	Email

Method of Payment ($20.00 minimum for credit card orders)

☐ Check (order shipped upon receipt) ☐ MasterCard
☐ Visa ☐ American Express

_____   _____
Card No. + 3-digit verification code (call if unsure of code)   Expiration Date
Signature